Masters of Perception
Sensory-Motor Integration in the Internal Martial Arts

Volume 3 of the Trilogy

Warriors Of Stillness
Meditative Traditions In The Chinese Martial Arts

Copyright © 2013 by Jan Diepersloot

Published by:
Qi Works
POB 369
Walnut Creek, CA 94597

Inquiries should be addressed to:

Jan Diepersloot/Qi Works
POB 369
Walnut Creek, CA 94597

E-mail may be addressed to:
jandiep@earthlink.net

Library of Congress Control Number: 2012914135

ISBN: 978-0-9859865-0-6

Cover, book design and illustrations by Adduci Studios.

This Work is Dedicated to
a Master of Perception,
my Shifu

衷心的感謝

Acknowledgments

To my editors, Ed Lempinen, Louis Swaim,
Greg Pass, Jean Vieth, and Paul Samberg:

I thank each of you for your unique contribution
in turning my tortured prose into readable English!

Thank you Adduci Studios, for the beautiful cover,
book design and illustrations.

Table of Contents

Personal Preface: Calvinism, Daoism, and the Creative Principle

Childhood Roots

I was born and raised in the belief of a Creator: omniscient, omnipresent and omnipotent, a supreme being somehow outside of and above nature who had created everything that exists. He was of a Calvinist bent, this creator, and although described as indescribable, the image that distilled in my mind, not surprisingly, was that of the cultural archetype: an old white man with a long white beard, in the mold of Michelangelo's Moses. For most of my childhood I pretty much accepted this belief without question; after all, it's to the parents that the child looks for an explanation of things, both cosmic and practical, and as long as things go along fairly well, there's no reason to question the explanations offered for the how and why of things.

But when I was 10, the first of several personal cosmic earthquakes struck the edifice of this belief system and reverberated to cause cracks in its foundation. As goalie on the soccer team, I caught a ball in the stomach, which ruptured my appendix. My parents being away for a rare weekend of rest and relaxation, and the domestic help dismissing my complaints, it was three days before I was taken to the hospital with a nearly fatal case of peritonitis. I spent a month in the hospital, but pulled through, the physical scars of my surgeries symbolic of the deeper emotional and spiritual wounds I sustained as a result of this trauma.

Feeling betrayed on some sort of cosmic level, I could not fathom why God decided to inflict this pain and suffering on me. What had I done to deserve that? Emotionally, I was unable to accept my parents' well-intentioned but ultimately self-defeating explanations that, even if we don't know the reason, we must believe that God did it for a reason and that God's reason is ultimately for our own good. Not even articulate enough to voice my doubts, I swallowed them, nodded and said, "Yes, of course," and continued on with life as usual. But the seeds of doubt and rebellion had been sown into my pre-adolescent heart and mind.

The second cosmic earthquake to shake me at the core came five years later when my father, just 52 years old, suffered a massive stroke and died. This event once more ignited my entire being with the most urgent questions of divine will and justice. And then, during the next seven years, when my old soccer injury required a series of surgeries to remove scar tissue that was inhibiting the function of my small intestine, my personal faith in the correctness of the church and its doctrines was further diminished.

From adolescence into young adulthood I lived in a vacuum of emotional and intellectual confusion. As a result, my college years in the 1960s became, essentially, a protracted personal search for meaning to put the shattered core of my psyche back together again and arrive at a worldview with some coherence. Along with the rejection of the church and its teachings, and a rejection of the conservative politics associated with church culture, the cosmic rage engendered a growing radicalization in my own politics.

The social and political crises of the 1960s provided an outlet for the anger and rage generated in me by my personal health and spiritual crises. Even as the existing social and political values were being questioned and exposed as corrupt, a new world of hope and justice beckoned in the birth of the counterculture. I shared a visceral sorrow and horror at the assassinations of John F. Kennedy, Martin Luther King, and Bobby Kennedy in a span of less than five years; I was swept up in the events of the Free Speech Movement, the civil rights movement, the antiwar movement, and the women's movement.

Graduate school saw the final and fitting resolution of my deteriorating relation with the church. I had stopped attending at all by then, and out of concern for the safety of my soul, the minister and some church elders traveled to visit me in my home. They put the question to me bluntly: "Do you accept Jesus Christ as your personal savior, or not?" My response was similarly blunt: "Since I do not believe in the existence of a supernatural Father, it seems futile to discuss the existence of a supernatural Son."

I did stress that I thought of Christ as a great moral teacher, but from their point of view that was not an adequate response and they left, clearly dismayed. Two weeks later, the church bulletin announced my excommunication.

Jumping ahead in order to come full circle, when people ask me these days what church I belong to or what my religion is, I tell them I belong to the Church of Creativity and I believe in the Creative Principle – a response that usually elicits a questioning look and further request to elaborate. I then explain my point of view that since in all cultures the first and greatest power universally attributed to the Divine is the power of creation, it follows that the proper realm of human religiosity is to participate and grow in the divine by developing and expressing our creative natures. I believe, in other words, that the purpose and meaning of a conscious life is simply to become an artist in every facet of it, making every act an act of creation that balances the yin and yang of things.

Adult World Views

Through my explorations in the mid-1960s, the religious codes and values of my youth, and even its explanation of the nature of reality, came to seem utterly inadequate. My belief in the Creator God was replaced by the belief in the Creative Principle; belief in religious doctrine was replaced by belief in the evidence of science and belief in the supernatural was replaced by belief in rationality.

And my new understanding of reality and its underpinnings was corroborated by my graduate studies in linguistics. Here I began to find a new insight into the structure of the universe. I became enthralled with the beauty and elegance of the binary oppositional principle as the underlying, universal structural mechanism of language. Thinking that the structure of language must reflect and express the structure of reality with a capital R, I began looking into other disciplines where research results corroborated the notion that the binary oppositional principle was the fundamental organizing principle of natural experience, and of nature itself: Piaget in psychology and Levi-Strauss in anthropology were developing fascinating theories of learning and kinship utilizing the binary principle as the organizing structural constant. Likewise, the formalization of the binary principle in mathematics and its application in the technology of computer science in the following decades proved further corroboration of the fundamental nature of the polarity principle.

In fields as diverse as psychology and physics, the principle of the "unity of opposites" was slowly gathering momentum as perhaps the greatest explanatory principle in the history of science. The psychologist Carl Jung employed with great success the polarity paradigm to explain the profound dynamics between the sexes. Jung paid explicit homage to Daoist yin-yang teachings on the interpenetration of opposites for his anima-animus theory on the structure of the human psyche.

As in psychology, so too in physics. As research into the furthest reaches of the material world and the structure of the atom deepened, it led the great twentieth century Danish physicist Niels Bohr to rediscover the ancient Daoist concept of polarity as the basic structure and creative principle of the universe and reality. Symbolic of this conceptual convergence of eastern and western modes of knowledge, when Bohr was knighted in 1947, he chose as his coat of arms the ancient Chinese yin-yang symbol and the inscription: *"Contraria sunt Complementa"* — Opposites are Complimentary (Fig. 1).[1]

Fig. 1
Bohr's Coat of Arms

...

My own introduction to Daoist thought and its philosophy of polarity occurred as a result of my taking up the practice of the Chinese internal martial arts in the mid-1970s to deal with recurring migraines. This proved a serendipitous decision in many ways.

---

[1] Fritjof Capra, *"The Tao of Physics: An Exploration of the Parallels Between Modern Physics and Eastern Mysticism,"* Shambhala, Boulder, CO, 1975, p. 160.

As I started reading the Daoist classics, I was moved by the discovery that these ancients had already thought deeply about polarity, and had in fact formulated an entire philosophy and way of life based on yin-yang polarity as the fundamental operating principle of the universe. In the famous circular yin-yang symbol, there's a white dot in the black and a black dot in the white (Fig. 2). In this small detail is the essence of the philosophy: all things contain the seed of their own opposite, and the mutual interpenetration of opposites drives change through time.

Fig. 2
Yin-Yang symbol

I began to recognize manifestations of this foundational idea in my study and practice of the internal martial arts. Soft could be more powerful than hard. Stillness could control movement. To someone of my background, these and other apparent contradictions posed by Daoism and the practice of the internal martial arts seemed deeply paradoxical. And while I found these paradoxes provocative, I also found it difficult to accept the claim that the slow and graceful movements of taijiquan (太極拳) were actually a powerful martial art. This skepticism turned into outright incredulity when I was introduced to the practice of standing meditation. How could simply standing still result in deadly powers and extraordinary martial skills, as was claimed? This phenomenon cried out for the spotlight of scrutiny, either to debunk it as fraud or come to an understanding how these claims could be true.

Meeting my Future Teacher

As I was growing up in the 1950s and struggling to find my way in the '60s and '70s, a continent away, the man who would eventually answer all these questions for me in the most definitive way possible and become the most influential of my future teachers, embarked on his own journey that would eventually lead towards a point of intersection with mine.

Master Sam Tam was born Tam Maan Yin (譚曼彥) in mainland China in 1940. There is no doubt in my mind that in the realm of martial arts, Master Tam fulfills all of the requirements of an "outlier" as described by Malcolm Gladwell in his book "Outliers."[2] Outliers, for Gladwell, are "people whose achievements fall outside normal experience." Their skills are so exceptional that it makes them fall outside of the bell curve of their profession. Tracing the rise and development of a diversity of greats in various fields, including Bill Gates, The Beatles, and a host of others, Gladwell comes to the conclusion that (1) innate predisposition or talent (2) combines with opportunity, as in a strongly supportive social environment, (3) to push a passionate temperament into an all consuming behavior.

Certainly all these factors can be readily observed in Master Tam's unique achievements in the martial arts generally, and in the internal martial arts particularly. The family history attests to his innate genetic endowment. Throughout the generations his family specialized in martial arts or medicine, and sometimes both. As his personality took shape, the emergence of the character traits necessary for outstanding achievement reinforced the genetic predisposition. Precocious as a child, Master Tam's character grew into a unique combination of intelligence, passion, perseverance, and competitiveness. Simply put, from an early age, Master Tam was determined to be the best at most everything.

Master Tam developed interest in martial arts very young. Lady Luck smiled on him, and opportunity came his way. In the late 1940s and in the early 50s his father, because of his occupation as a doctor in the Chinese armed forces, was able to arrange instruction for his son from high level military martial art instructors. Besides his native talent and fearless spirit, one trait that endeared Master Tam to his teachers was the great respect and deference Master Tam showed them. Because of this, and because they recognized his unique talents, each teacher pointed him to the next teacher he should seek out.

In the process he acquired a truly encyclopedic knowledge, both theoretical and practical, in the Chinese martial arts. Even to this day, I do not have the full picture of whom he studied with, or what and when, but amongst the most important in his career were certainly the following: Lau Fat Mang (劉法孟) (Eagle Claw), Han Xingyuan (韓星垣) (Yiquan, Xingyiquan, Baguazhang), Yu Pengxi (尤彭熙), (Yiquan),

---

[2] Malcolm Gladwell, "*Outliers*", Little, Brown and Company, New York, 2008.

Chang Dongshen (常東昇) (Shuaijiao), Zhang Xiang Wu (Taijiquan, Xingyiquan, Baguazhang) and Qi Jiangtao (綦江濤) (Taijiquan).

In the mid-1950s, a new chapter started in Master Tam's life, as the family emigrated to Canada. After a few years in Toronto, he married and moved to Vancouver B.C. where he raised his family. In the 60s he started to come down to the San Francisco Bay Area on a regular basis to visit friends and relatives. In the San Francisco martial arts community, Master Tam's reputation spread quickly (Fig. 3). Among his peers, he was respected for the breath and depth of his martial knowledge, and feared as a ferocious fighter who could enjoy instilling terror in his opponents.

...

It was during the 1970s that my own path intersected with Master Tam's for the first time. During that time I was studying in Berkeley with Fong Ha, Master Tam's friend and *shidi* (師弟), or younger brother in martial arts, especially yiquan.

Fig. 3
Master Tam as a young martial artist

As a consequence, Master Tam would periodically come down from Vancouver and visit. It was during these visits that I made his acquaintance and began to come to know him.

To tell the truth, on first meeting Master Tam, I didn't like him all that much. I was turned off by the stories of martial prowess that were told about him. And his demeanor seemed to me to corroborate this reputation. Though he was unfailingly polite and correct, his bearing expressed a confidence in his martial abilities that at times seemed to border on intimidation. Whether with friends or foes, he never left any doubt that, if provoked, he could do serious damage in a very short time.

Why the negative reaction on my part? I was on the rebound from the turbulence of the cultural and political revolutions of the 1960s and 1970s, and in true hippie fashion, all I wanted to do was meditate, practice taiji (太極), and seek the peaceful life. Sam Tam's reputation did not square with those goals, and so I tended to dismiss him as irrelevant to my own path. It didn't help that, in a number of ways, Sam seemed very dismissive of those of us who studied with Master Fong.

For one thing, he was always being picked up and whisked away by other very serious martial arts types for important and secretive consultations, to which we lowly white ghosts were not invited. At other times he would emerge from Master Fong's house, and, without coming over or saying a word, he would just watch us practice our routines in the park across the street, and then turn around and walk back into the house. Of course there was so much back then that I didn't see, or didn't understand. Only decades later did he tell me that he turned away because he couldn't bear watching how badly we were mangling the forms.

From the early 1980s till the late 1990s I had very little contact with Master Tam. He stopped coming down from Vancouver to visit martial arts friends and groups in the Bay Area. The reason, he explained later, was that at that point he had begun to realize that in order to master the taiji principle and the philosophy of yielding, he would have to give up all his old ways of using strength. Embarking on the quest for mastery of yielding and the method of expressing power without force, he entered, along with a few trusted friends, a period of ever deepening personal search and research into the relationship between meditation and martial arts.

Signing on to No-Force

Then, in 1996, a friend phoned to tell me that Sam Tam was in town again and that we were invited to an informal get together. Of course I decided to go, but to be honest, my continuing negative feelings towards him coupled with a deep loyalty to my teacher at the time, Master Cai Songfang (蔡松芳), left me with deep skepticism and disbelief about the descriptions of Sam Tam's new-found abilities that had filtered down through the gossip pipelines.

That night, as Master Tam demonstrated "no force"[3] and moved people around at will with apparent effortlessness, I couldn't help but be impressed. When it came my turn, I was determined to put up a struggle. But when I tried, I could not. While his hands were touching me, I experienced no push; I did not feel that I had been moved, and yet I had moved! It was only a couple of inches, but the experience left me profoundly puzzled.

The next year, along with some comrades, I went to visit him in Vancouver. It was a most memorable meeting. In theoretical and practical terms, he discussed and demonstrated his newfound skills of yielding and softness. It was one of the most concise lecture demonstrations of the internal martial arts and its principles that I have ever seen and heard. Just as striking, these newfound skills of yielding and softness seemed inextricably connected with a shift in personal outlook and attitude. Clearly, the taiji principle and philosophy had transformed him. He was less imposing and threatening, more friendly and engaging, and this allowed his impish sense of humor to guide his words and actions.

As my friends and I experienced that evening, and as countless others have experienced since, Master Tam's humor is an extension of his commitment to softness—and it is an excellent teaching tool. With easy confidence and a promise not to use force, he invited us to try to defeat him. The result? An evening of hilarity, with so much laughter that we were weak in the knees. No matter what we tried, each of us wound up doing one of three things: (1) losing balance and falling; (2) being immobilized to the point of paralysis; or (3) bouncing like a ball thrown against the wall. And through it all, Master Tam did not exhibit the slightest use of force or even a trace of physical effort.

Over the next few years in the late 90s, as I had more frequent occasion to observe and experience Master Tam both in workshops and in private interaction, I was forced to revise my previous feelings about him. I found myself in a quandary. Master Cai had returned to China, and it was unlikely that he would come back to California or that I would be able to visit him often in China.

---

[3] "No Force" here is not synonomous with "no touch"; Master Tam was touching us, but not using force to move us.

And then, I came to an important realization: when pushing hands with Master Cai and Master Tam, either could render me helpless. But there was a difference in the feeling of their hands. When Master Cai bounced me, I could feel force in his hands; when Master Tam bounced me, I felt no force at all. I did feel *something*, and that *something* seemed mysterious, elusive, even otherworldly. I wanted it.

Reluctantly then, I did the obvious thing. Putting aside my ego and previous negative sentiments, I asked Master Tam to accept me as his student - which he did, lightly, and with an easy smile. Then and there he used the internal martial arts to turn me from an enemy into a friend, a skeptic into a believer, a challenger into a student.

By now I've known Master Tam for over 30 years, and have been working closely with him as his student for over 15 years. During this latter period, as he became more and more well-known globally, he began drawing into his orbit a large number of accomplished martial artists from around the world who wanted to learn his signature softness. Thus I've been privileged to observe the transformation in Master Tam from a shifu (師父), meaning teacher, into a dashi (大師), meaning "big teacher" or the teacher of teachers.

Personally, as Master Tam's student for so many years, my exposure to his sensitivity and skill has been instrumental in realizing my own potential in the internal martial arts. Without his peerless instruction and his unyielding insistence on doing things the right way, I could never have realized the vision I had when I started my internal martial arts journey more than 35 years ago as of this writing: simply to rise to a level of mastery in the art that would bring me a sense of completion, fulfillment and happiness in my older years. I have that sense now. I have found and tasted the well-spring of life and it was—and is—in me. I have tasted the nectar of qi, and have begun to feel the power of the soft and yielding.

This raises the question of where to find the words to describe the experience and how to draw the map to the territory? Master Tam always emphasizes that the internal martial arts represents a special case of embodiment of the yin-yang principle. And indeed his teachings have reinforced in me a keen personal appreciation that polarity (Dao (道)=yin (陰)/yang (陽)) is the principle that underlies the unfolding of life itself.

Accordingly, it seemed only proper to make the polarity principle the underlying scaffolding for the structure of the experiences, observations, analyses and syntheses that have become this volume.

Additionally, for my entire life I have been a voracious reader, so even before I met Master Tam, and long before I became his student, it was my nature to complement my internal martial arts experience by research into anatomy, physiology, psychology, kinesiology and neuroscience. This life-long habit of questing figures prominently in this volume and has made its methodology at once subjective and objective, phenomenological and empirical, participatory and observational. My search and research since I began this quest in 1976 has ranged widely over western and eastern knowledge; the result is a synthesis that I hope offers clear, though perhaps sometimes unconventional, perspectives on the interactions of stillness and movement, body and mind.

Overview: The Four Stages of Development[4]

The Qi Stage

During the qi (氣) stage, internal martial artists work to realize the potential of their genetic endowment by developing their physical constitution. The primary principles internal martial artists follow to cultivate robust health in the qi state are proper posture, proper breath and proper mindset. In the internal martial arts, the rules of posture are governed by the pivotal concept of zhongding (中定), or central equilibrium, and consist of the optimal re-alignment of the spine in the vertical plane.

Within this proper postural framework, internal martial artists utilize mindful breathing practices to transform typical (and usually restricted) breathing patterns into full and free natural breathing. As this process unfolds over time, the tensions that stiffen and harden us, both physically and mentally, progressively dissolve. The resulting state of relaxation is called song (鬆) by the Chinese, and denotes a state of alert relaxation that is ready for immediate action.

Proper breath and proper posture create the foundation for optimally efficient movement of torso and limbs. The rules for movement, like posture, also are dictated by the constraints of central equilibrium. The fundamental components, or basic grammar, of movement are the horizontal, vertical and rotational movements of the body's central vertical axis in space. These three elemental movements combine to create an infinite number of possible movements.

In the qi stage, internal martial artists learn to nurture a state of glowing health in which deep and easy breathing, optimal balance, fluid movement and li (力), meaning basic strength, become the building blocks for the development of jin (勁), or power.

---

[4] The inspiration and basis for this overview was a lecture on "Qi and Qi Gong" given by Master SamTam in 2007 during a summer retreat in Santa Barbara, CA.

The Jin Stage

Through further specialized qigong training, practitioners can refine and distill the li, the basic physical strength derived from qigong practice, into the martial skills of jin, a refined type of martial power, sometimes also called fajin. Li is the sort of strength used in pushing a stalled car. It is linear and uses the force of momentum. Jin, as we will see, is a special kind of non-linear power discharged from the body's abdominal center, called the dantian (丹田) in Chinese.

Most martial arts apply force by leaning the body and/or exerting the segmented strength of the appendages. The metaphor is the reality: an attack is "launched," a punch is "thrown," a kick is "extended." Because their power derives from momentum and is therefore external to the organism, these martial arts are properly called external martial arts.

Jin, as the refinement of li, is based on the principle of central equilibrium. Maintaining central equilibrium at all times, along with utterly controlled economy of movement, allows the dantian to become functional as the focus for cultivation and storage of the qi. When issued, this qi becomes jin, the explosive expression of the integrated strength of the body. Jin has enormous power but paradoxically it has no momentum. Its expression is explosively spherical, equal in all directions.

The internal martial art of Yiquan teaches us that the training that accomplishes this spherical explosiveness is called "six directions training." It is first practiced separately in each dimension — up-down, front-back, and left-right — but eventually entails the simultaneous expansion from the center in all six directions. Thus jin, or fajin as it is also called, can be thought of as a pulse of energy and force generated at the body's center that may be discharged from any point on the body's periphery. I will describe how the essential method used by internal martial artists to train both center and periphery in developing the skill of fajin is the ever-deepening exploration of breathing practices.

The diaphragm is key. It acts as a central piston in the generation of both qi and jin. The diaphragm connects with and engages with the lungs above it to create qi; in connecting with and engaging the abdominal cavity, it begins to generate jin.

Internal martial artists aim to acquire conscious control over diaphragmatic action by means of "reverse" breathing techniques. Fundamental in this process is learning how to control the contraction of the diaphragm to regulate the internal hydraulic pressure in the abdominal cavity.

With time and effective practice, the dantian — located roughly 1.5 inches below the navel and 1.5 inches into the belly — is transformed into a "dome of power." It becomes sensitive, subtly responsive, at one instant soft and pliable, and in the next hard as steel.

The Yi Stage

Yi (意) is generally translated as intent, or even more broadly speaking, imagination or consciousness. The yi, in other words, is our executive agency, the decision-maker in us that resides in the frontal lobes of the brain. It is the yi that considers the possible voluntary movements and decides which to allow and which to put on hold. It is also the yi that instructs our musculature as to the when and how to proceed with the execution of an allowed activity.

Within the internal martial arts context, the training and development of central equilibrium, breathing skills and jin, are all functions of the yi. But the stage of yi for internal martial artists is more narrowly defined by two criteria, a practitioner's ability to (1) generate the jin power internally, through mental intent and without external movement, and (2) discharge it (in)to the opponent from any point on the body that is in contact with the opponent.

But yet, translating yi as intention captures only half of its meaning. Underlying all voluntary motor decisions and actions is a perceptual substrate; that is, actions and movements are based on perceptions of the external environment.

And it is precisely in the frontal lobes of the brain, where the yi resides, that the integration of the sensory and motor components of the nervous system takes place and results in voluntary action. The yi, then, is the neurological interface between the sensory and the motor components of the nervous system. Like the head and tail sides of a coin, the yi is a polarity structure where attention and perceptual awareness is the yin to the yang of intention and motor activity.

Solitary standing meditation and taijiquan practice are effective in training this perceptual awareness; they build balance and proprioception (internal perception of the relationships between bones, muscles, and connective tissue), vision and hearing. Moreover, martial arts are a contact sport, and the "soft" internal styles emphasize tactile sensitivity over force. The tactile sense is broadened and deepened by means of the practice of partnered exercises, such as "pushing hands" patterns and techniques.

Through pushing hands practice, internal martial artists develop the sensory skills of ting (聽) or listening, zou (走) or yielding, and zhan-nian (粘 黏) or adhering -sticking, which altogether result in a lighter, subtler touch. Coupled with song (relaxation), zhongding (stability) and integration acquired through solitary standing meditation and form practice, this greater tactile awareness allows us, on the one hand, to develop the ability to hijack an opponent's central equilibrium, while on the other, to prevent the opponent from doing it to us.

These pushing-hand skills derive their power from their ability to transform intention into attention and force into no force; they take internal martial artists beyond the power of jin and yi to the sensitivity and responsiveness of shen.

The Shen Stage

Just as the yi can be understood as a polarity structure of intention (yang) and attention (yin), attention itself is also a polarity structure: perceptual attention is always somewhere along a spectrum of hard focus (yang) to soft focus (yin).

The yi utilizes the hard-focused attention to execute its intent, and guide our motor movement. By definition, hard-focused attention is detail-oriented and partial. It is the soft-focus perception, however, that is the foundational basis for the development of shen (神), the ultimate level of attainment in the internal martial arts, usually simply translated as "spirit" or more descriptively, as the "spirit of awareness" or the "spirit of enlightenment."

As the ultimate level of comprehensive holistic sensory awareness, one cultivates Shen through the systematic relaxation training of both the internal senses of balance and proprioception and the external senses of touch, vision and hearing. As the senses learn to relax, the more they soften their focus, the more they expand the range of their perception. This is true for each sense individually, but also for all the senses collectively. Shen is the combined information/data from all the expanded senses together that is integrated into the one, overall, simultaneous perception of our surrounding environment.

The internal martial arts path and its stages are part and parcel of the broader and deeper current of Chinese culture and consciousness that is Daoism. The Daoist prescription for appropriate action in the world, that is, how to get to the shen level, is the path of wuwei (無為). Literally meaning "not doing," wuwei is perhaps more fully described as the way to mastery of any skill by "minimizing effort through maximizing awareness."

Throughout the ages, Pao Ding, the lowly kitchen worker described by Zhuangzi, frequently is cited as a paragon of enlightenment, representing the embodiment and pinnacle of this philosophy.[5] Pao Ding, through decades of practice, developed the ability to dress a carcass without ever dulling his knife. When his Lord the Duke queried him about this extraordinary skill, Pao Ding explained to him: "What I care about is the Way, which goes beyond skill. When I first began cutting up oxen, all I could see was the ox itself. After three years, I no longer saw the whole ox. And now — now I go at it by spirit and don't look with my eyes. Perception and understanding have come to a stop and spirit [shen] moves where it wants."

Pao Ding's description shows the way of wuwei and shen for any artist: from the initial use of brute force informed by limited perception one progresses to using refined force guided by precise focus (yi) until finally one becomes capable of using the no-force of encompassing awareness (shen). Whether it's carving up carcasses, playing a musical instrument, or controlling an opponent, at the highest stage of shen the tools become an extension of the body; one feels and senses with them to achieve flow with, rather than intervention in, the surrounding world.

Achievement in the internal martial arts is ultimately measured by how close martial artists come to the ideal of "awareness overcoming strength." The journey of developing these sensory skills is a deeply transformative process. It involves, in every aspect of life, the overcoming and restructuring of deeply seated and practically hard-wired patterns of using force in reaction to threat and challenge. Over time, the sensory perceptual skills and their associated motor skills take root as the new operating system that runs our bodies and minds. Then, gradually, a shift in perspective and character occurs, guiding us away from egocentrism and competitiveness into a state of open-mindedness and tranquility.

---

[5] There are many versions of this story. In this work, I will cite the version told and interpreted by Kuang-Ming Wu in "The Butterfly as Companion: Meditations on the First Three Chapters of the Chuang Tzu," State University of New York Press, New York, 1990.

簿一

Book 1
The Mindful Body
Somatic Functions Controlled by Mental Faculties

Introduction to Book 1

The Anatomy of Posture and Movement

The martial arts, of course, have always had an abiding interest in movement, both in how it is generated and how it is controlled. Historically, many martial arts styles were created based on characteristic movements of a variety of animals, such as tiger, bear, crane, snake, etc. Master Wang Xiangzhai (王薌齋), the founder of the internal martial art style of standing meditation presented in this work, criticized such efforts to create martial arts styles based on animal behaviors. He instead sought to develop a martial art that exploits the specific human characteristics of our upright posture and bipedal gait by turning the vulnerability into the very foundation and strength of the underlying concepts of posture and movement.

In living organisms mobility requires stability. Hence evolution has favored the stable quadruped solution adopted by most mammals. Certainly the quadruped posture and means of locomotion is more stable than the bipedal posture and gait primates adopted when they came down from the trees and starting living life on the savanna. For primates, then, adopting bipedal posture and movement must have offered both immediate and long-term, lasting advantages.

The adaptation to bipedal movement occurred 4-6 million years ago in an east African landscape that was getting dryer and dryer. With forests giving way to grasslands, what benefits did the permanent upright posture offer? Initially, for the early grassland hominid, being upright was not about walking, but rather about posture when foraging. The height inherent in an upright posture allowed our ancestors to see over tall grass and to identify and intimidate predators and other hominids. Likewise, with the hands freed, they gained better ability to climb vertical tree trunks and to reach and pull down the low-hanging, fruit-laden branches.

Freed hands were also indispensable for carrying food, offspring and tools when our ancestors were on the move. And move they did. They ran for a living, running game down by following until it tired out, sometimes days later. Their upright posture helped reduce heat stress by limiting the body surface area exposed to the savannah's intense tropical sun and heat. Further adaptations, including hairlessness, sweat glands, and other physical features helped our ancestors become capable of running long distances in the open sun near the equator.

The adaptation process to erect walking, visualized so stunningly by Rudolph Zalinger in his "March of Progress"[6] sequence (Fig. 4), changed the skeletal structure profoundly. On top, for the skull to balance on the spinal column,

Fig. 4
Zaliger's "March of Progress"

the foramen magnum (the hole in the skull through which the spinal cord attaches to the brain) had to shift position and become centered at the bottom of the skull. In the middle, an S-curve developed in the spine to support the weight of the upper body in a flexible manner. And at bottom, the pelvic structure's conjunction of thigh bones and hip sockets evolved to carry the stress and weight associated with bipedal locomotion.

This process reached a culmination of sorts when the primate line that ultimately led to the human form began to diverge from the apes. Evolution of permanent bipedal posture and locomotion not only freed the hands, but in combination with the evolution of the opposable thumb, set the evolutionary stage for the simultaneous development of toolmaking and language. These developments culminated in the explosive growth of the cerebral cortex in the pleistocene era about half a million years ago.

---

[6] Wikipedia, Rudolph Zalinger, "March of Progress."

At the same time, evolution towards permanent bipedal posture and locomotion placed increasingly enormous demands on those parts of the central nervous system involved with balance. As a result, the cerebellum, the organ most concerned with balance and proprioception, also underwent explosive growth and development to meet the neural demand for processing power. Thus the primate nervous system evolved: from lesser to greater ability to perceive the environment; from lesser to greater ability to learn from that experience; from lesser to greater ability to respond to and move around in the environment; and ultimately, from lesser to greater control over the environment.

For the internal martial artist, standing meditation becomes no less than the conscious practice of this evolutionary impulse. Standing meditation practice brings the mostly unconscious functions of the cerebellum, namely bipedal balance and proprioception, to awareness in the frontal lobes of the neocortex. By cultivating greater awareness of the internal environment, that is, the perception of the whole-body self around its central equilibrium, the internal martial artist gains a two-fold advantage over any opponent. Not only does this awareness enhance her own postural stability and movement agility, but it also allows her to understand, and exploit the weaknesses in her opponent's posture and movements.

...

Bone, muscle and connective tissue combine into a structure that maintains our posture and creates our movement. In the human body, the bones function as rigid compression members, while the muscles and connective tissue are the flexible tensional members that act upon the bones to maintain posture and create movement.

Our bones are joined in many different ways, but what all joints have in common is their function as mechanical fulcrums that allow the bones to act as levers upon each other. In the lever principle, a force is applied to a weight via a pivot point or fulcrum. In the body, bones are the levers, joints are the fulcrums or pivot points, and force is supplied by the muscles and mediated by the connective tissue.

Because of the nature of our joints, most human movement has to do with the extension and flexion of both the trunk and the extremities. To maintain posture and create movement within this context, the muscles must work in pairs that are functionally antithetical and complimentary to each other, so that when one contracts, the other relaxes and is stretched. Examples are the hamstrings and quadriceps that act as extensors and flexors of the legs, or the triceps and biceps which act as extensors and flexors of the arms. When you contract the biceps, the triceps rests and the arm flexes. When you contract the triceps, the biceps rests and the arm extends. Generally, the muscle that causes a movement to occur by contracting is referred to as the agonist, while the resting muscle is called the antagonist. Thus depending on which initiates the movement, both extensors and flexors can be either agonist or antagonist.

The 206 separate bones of our body are each part of a whole and act in their totality as one skeleton. By the same logic the more than 600 muscles that act upon the bones to maintain posture and produce movement also can be considered as each being a part of a whole. In their totality, these 600 muscles can be seen to act as one muscle, or rather two opposing muscles that constitute a yin-yang pair. Several facts argue in favor of such an interpretation. First, it takes an incredible amount of muscle synergy to maintain posture and movement. Even a simple movement engages most of the body's muscles, allowing an infinite number of possible simultaneous and/or sequential muscle contractions. Moreover, a single muscle may contract or lengthen any number of its fibers individually or collectively in order to change its configuration and shape in an almost amoeba-like fashion. These and related facts have led modern scholars such as Deane Juhan to conclude that "... the body [has] only one muscle ... that can contract or extend any number of its millions of fibers and utilize all of its bony levers and tendon attachments to achieve an infinite variation of shapes ... there is only one muscle, controlled by one mind."[7]

As with bones and muscles, so it is with connective tissue. We have innumerable types of connective tissues that in their totality constitute the one connective tissue.

---

[7] Deane Juhan, "*Job's Body: A Handbook for Bodywork,*" Station Hill Press, Barrytown, New York, 1987, pp. 113-15.

Each muscle, each visceral organ, all blood and lymph vessels and nerves are encased in specialized connective tissue wrapping, also called fascia. All are connected by and into a ubiquitous web that supports, enwraps, and separates all the functional units of the body. For this reason, modern scholars increasingly consider the numerous types of specialized connective tissues collectively as the one "organ of form" or the "organ of structure" because functionally, connective tissue supports and maintains the relative positions of the various organs and muscles and skeletal structures in the body.

While in posture and movement the muscles provide the active force that acts on the rigid bones, the connective tissue is the underlying and all-encompassing passive matrix that contains and supports both the bones and the muscles. In other words, the structural integrity of the body as a whole depends on the balance of the various connective tissues (tendons, ligaments, strings, cords and fascial sheets) that hold the bones, muscles and organs in relationship to each other.

It's important to realize how connective tissue and muscles have opposing but complimentary functions in the maintenance of posture and creating movement. Muscle strength is active and contractile in nature, while connective tissue strength is passive and elastic in nature. The muscles adjust the tension levels in the tendons and fascia necessary to maintain posture and produce movement. The crucial point here is that as muscle stretches the tendons, fascia and other components of the connective tissue web, the web, due to its elastic nature, stores energy that is used to partially power subsequent actions.

Fig. 5
Kangaroo Locomotion

To understand better how this works, consider the kangaroo's bipedal hopping method of locomotion. The kangaroo (Fig. 5) has developed tremendously powerful elastic tendons in its legs. These tendons are so efficient in absorbing and storing energy that up to 80% of the energy generated by gravity each time the kangaroo lands is used to power the next jump. This means that the faster and higher and further the kangaroo jumps, its energy consumption actually increases in efficiency. In other words, relatively speaking, at higher speeds, it needs to use less muscle energy to cover long distances.

The relevance of all this to the internal martial arts is defined by the methodology these arts employ to make the unconscious conscious. The reality is that the one skeleton, the one muscle and the one connective tissue together constitute one body that is controlled by one nervous system. But this nervous system has two parts, conscious and subconscious. In fact, most of our daily interactions with people are governed by subconscious processes; we simply are unaware of them and our responses to provocations are limited by this lack of awareness. Standing meditation is the antidote for this lack of awareness. It makes the conscious pursuit of unified body and mind central to internal martial arts strategy, tactics and practices.

Consequently, the relationship between stillness (standing meditation) and movement is of paramount importance for the internal martial artist. Understanding this relationship thoroughly will optimize both offensive and defensive strategies, their tactical implementation, and the training programs based on them. A lack of understanding will lead to deficient offensive and defensive strategies, erroneous tactical implementation, and inadequate training programs.

Though posture is often thought of as stillness as opposed to movement, actually our posture must be considered a type of movement also. In other words, the stillness we are talking about is not the stillness of death as opposed to the movement of life. It is not the comparative stillness of plants as opposed to the movements of animals. It is not the (relative) stillness of sleep, not the stillness of couch potato TV-watching, not the stillness of paralysis, not the stillness of passed out stupor, nor any other stillness in which the machinery for movement and its controlling mechanism have been fully or partially shut down. No, the stillness we cultivate in our standing (postural) meditation entails readiness, a stillness that is pregnant with possibilities for movement. It is the stillness of the deer ready to bolt and flee, the stillness of the tiger ready to pounce. The stillness we are talking about, in other words, is movement not yet released. It is the stillness of potential movement as opposed to actual movement. In this stillness, awareness enables us to respond to our environment rather than react to it.

In the external martial arts, as well as most western sports, the training emphasis is on building muscle strength. In the internal martial arts, however, we emphasize cultivating the elastic strength of the connective tissue web and utilize muscle effort to that end. We cultivate the elastic nature of our body frame in order to be able to absorb our opponent's energy and repel her effortlessly. Here the energy stored by the tendons and connective tissue web is not that of gravity and falling, but is the opponent's own energy. When our connective tissue web is stretched elastically (by the opponent's force), its recoil bounces the opponent back, much like a trampoline. Considering that compared with the kangaroo, human tendon energy storage capacity is a paltry 15-20 percent, we would do well to learn how to use our muscles intelligently to stretch, lengthen and strengthen the energy storage capacity (elasticity) of the fascial web that literally holds us together.

Part 1
On Qí
Cultivating Health

Chapter 1: Standing Meditation

The Origin and Purpose of Standing Meditation

Historically, most martial arts have delivered force through movement. On the most basic and common level, it is the momentum of movement that generates the power in the martial arts; we fight by throwing a punch or launching a kick. Because this type of force is not generated in or by the internal center, the martial arts that use these methods came to be called external martial arts.

Chinese warrior-sages discovered two great drawbacks to this method of delivering force. First, if the movement misses the intended target, the momentum causes the fighter to overextend and lose balance, putting her in a dangerous situation. Second, the force derived from momentum is partial. While the force of a fist in a punch or of the foot in a kick can be powerful indeed, neither is as great as the force generated by the body acting as a whole unit.

Through analysis and experimentation, these ancients solved both problems by discovering how to generate force from stillness. In this highly sophisticated method, a pulse of power is generated in stillness from the center of the body and discharged into the opponent at the point of contact. Because it radiates out spherically from a center, this force (1) has no momentum and (2) is holistic, not partial. Not only is the force more powerful but it also reduces or eliminates the risk that a fighter will lose balance.

These ideas evolved in a few martial arts systems, such as xingyiquan (形意拳) and taijiquan that collectively became known as the neijia quan, or the family of the internal martial arts. Historically, then, a large part of the curriculum of internal martial arts systems entailed practicing stillness while holding many different postures, each one functionally designed for a different purpose or situation.

The late nineteenth and early twentieth century era was a time of great social and political upheaval in China, and fed a great renaissance in the martial arts. A myriad of martial arts styles and systems flourished as a way to protect the nation and strengthen the character and resolve of the people.

From this renaissance emerged the genius of Master Wang Xiangzhai (王薌齋) (Fig. 6) who lived from 1885 until 1963 and synthesized all these different systems of postural practices into one universal meditation posture. His method of zhanzhuang standing meditation must be acknowledged as the ultimate refinement and culmination of the Chinese martial arts.

Fig. 6
Wang Xiangzhai

When the communists came to power in China in the mid-twentieth century, a decision was made on a national level to emphasize the health aspects of martial arts and de-emphasize their martial and spiritual aspects, transforming them into more athletic health arts and acrobatic performance arts. The latter part of the twentieth century also saw the increasing exportation of the martial arts from China, introducing and popularizing them all over the world.

The effect of this diffusion of internal martial arts development in the modern era, both in China and worldwide, has been largely negative. The postural practices of the internal martial arts have deteriorated and the concept of internal power has become the stuff of legend rather than of cultivation.

Increasingly practiced solely as a means of health maintenance rather than for martial skills, the internal martial arts have all but abandoned postural practices in favor of movement practice. In the process, they have largely lost their essence, their soul, and instead have come to look like watered-down dance versions of the external martial arts.

Yet despite these developments, the real internal martial arts have not been lost altogether. Pockets of knowledge and cultivation of the old skills of internal power continue to exist and some adherents continue to spread the true art. It has been my incredibly good fortune to connect with a few teachers who were still familiar with the old ways.

My Introduction to Standing Meditation

My own introduction to standing meditation was a rough one. My teacher, Master Fong Ha, had brought his teacher, Master Han Xingyuan (Fig. 7), from Hong Kong to the San Francisco Bay Area to conduct a course. Master Han was a teacher of the old school who applied the "sink or swim" principle to his teaching methods.

Fig. 7
Master Han Xingyuan

His standing meditation classes were strenuous, to say the least. Students stood, with their arms held in a circle in front of the chest, for a minimum of 45 minutes that often stretched to over an hour. Students sometimes were sweating so profusely that the ground around their feet actually became wet. Rumor had it that Master Han did not dismiss class until a sufficient number of sweat puddles had accumulated. At times legs would get so tired that the students would begin shaking uncontrollably. Or their arms would become so heavy that the students could not hold them up any longer and inadvertently lowered them — only to have Master Han walk over and raise those arms back to the more tortuous position. But worse than the physical strain was the intellectual-emotional anguish of following the credo of "do as you're shown and don't ask any questions." For many of the more highly educated and concept-driven students, including myself, doing things without really understanding why was the worst kind of torture. Whether this is the ideal method for transmitting the wonders of standing meditation is debatable. Certainly it was a reflection of a different culture and time.

Historically, the traditional Chinese manner of transmitting the martial arts through the generations often subjected students to rigorous endurance trials designed to test their desire and loyalty. It definitely served as an effective filtering mechanism to separate out those without sufficient endurance. Hearing of Master Han's fame and reputation, many came and tried while he was in the San Francisco Bay Area. I was one of the few who stayed – both because I realized it was a testing situation and I could be as stubborn as the next person, and because of the support of fellow students.

From my own teaching experience, I've come to a different conclusion about the best way to guide a student's progress forward. I believe it is through a series of small steps that incrementally push the student to higher levels of achievement. Furthermore, in my experience, students progress faster when they are given a conceptual framework that defines the goals of the postural practice, and describes the feelings and sensations they are likely to encounter in the process. And although he did not follow this practice when teaching our group, in the final analysis, it appears Master Han also subscribed to this point of view. Once, when he was asked how long one should stand, he answered, "It's better to stand correctly for one minute than to stand incorrectly for one hour."

Standing Meditation for Health and Martial Art

It seems the simplest thing, standing still. But when you actually try it, and pay close attention, it's not that easy. The "still" part, especially, becomes very difficult the longer one tries to do it. One always seems to be moving a little bit, involuntarily shifting a little bit from heel to toe, or from left to right foot, twitching a little here, itching a little there.

Because in a fight, any involuntary movement represents an opening that can be attacked by the opponent, standing meditation seeks to do away with all involuntary movement, and to make any and all movement strictly voluntary, i.e., an act of awareness and will.

The method of standing meditation leads students to become still by first becoming aware of all their involuntary movement and then, as such movement occurs, minimizing it through relaxation and intent. Moreover, in conjunction with postural realignment, standing meditation utilizes natural breathing methods to cultivate the simultaneous relaxation and integration of the motor and sensory systems.

The stillness thus cultivated is not a passive state of inaction in which the motor system is switched off. On the contrary, this stillness constitutes an active readiness to move in any direction, with full awareness and control over the body's central equilibrium. Literally, such stillness is the foundation for both the offensive and defensive skills of the internal martial arts.

While it may take years of standing meditation practice to achieve mastery of its martial applications and implications, a whole range of the health benefits becomes available much sooner. Neurologically, standing meditation works first and foremost on the functions of the cerebellum. These are the internal senses of (1) balance and (2) proprioception (the internal perception of one's body parts). These senses usually are taken for granted and operate largely below the level of our awareness. Generally, we are not aware of our balance until we lose it, and likewise we don't consciously perceive the structural and functional relationship of one body part to another.

Standing meditation, as demonstrated by Master Tam (Fig. 8), unifies balance and proprioception and brings them to the fore-ground of our awareness. With time, it reintegrates the various parts of our muscular, skeletal and connective tissue systems around a precisely aligned vertical axis. This leads us to a new awareness of the relationships of these systems within the context of the body's central equilibrium.

Fig. 8
Master Sam Tam

On a social level, standing meditation offers itself as an antidote for the stresses and strains imposed on the individual by life in contemporary society. Modern life simultaneously imposes the stress of chronic and prolonged sympathetic excitation on its participants, depleting the body's store of energy reserves, while suppressing the parasympathetic nervous system and its restorative functions.[8] This disruption of the basic functional polarity of the autonomic nervous system is evident in the widespread sub- or malfunction of the vegetative systems in so many people today.

In this context, the restorative effects of standing meditation derive from the effect of its postural and breathing methods on the autonomic nervous system. Standing mediation promotes the rebalancing of the two branches of the autonomic nervous system. The practice of stillness of body and tranquility of mind simultaneously inhibits the chronically activated sympathetic nervous system and stimulates the parasympathetic nervous system.

In this way, then, standing meditation is a cure for the "stress" civilization inflicts on us: its practice leads to improvement of our basic vegetative functions. As our digestive, reproductive, circulatory and respiratory systems function more and more robustly, we come to enjoy the good health and increased vitality levels of the qi stage.

---

[8] We will explore this in greater detail in a later chapter, but briefly, the autonomic nervous has two complementary and opposing branches: the sympathetic and parasympathetic nervous systems. The sympathetic branch and its associated hormonal system marshals and uses the body's energetic resources for periods of activity in general, and for crises in particular. The parasympathetic branch and its associated hormonal system replenishes our energy during periods of inactivity and rest. It optimizes and regulates the vegetative functions of digestion, reproductive, circulation and respiration.

Chapter 2: Integrating Posture, Breath and Awareness in Stillness and Movement

Gravity Lines West and East

Fig. 9 is a skeletal chart like many that grace the office walls of your local doctor or chiropractor. The image shows the line of gravity, or centerline, of a human body as it hangs from a hook attached to a fixed ceiling. Seeing the chart in the waiting room at my medical practitioner's office for many years, and being much interested in the nature of movement, for a while I had a slightly morbid fascination with this image. At some point I began to wonder if the human being so depicted was dead or alive.

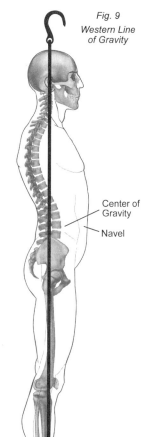

Fig. 9 Western Line of Gravity

Center of Gravity

Navel

Heel

Western Line of Gravity (Centerline)

I eventually came to the conclusion that most probably he was dead meat, to use the vernacular. For one thing, the body is hanging there, and there's no floor to support the feet – a difficult feat for anyone to do for any length of time and live. So what we're seeing here is the vertical line of gravity, not of a living human being but of an inanimate and inert object. Indeed, the body's general look and the position of the feet in particular, indicate the body has been dead for a while, stiffened by freezing or rigor mortis, or both. The angle of the feet indicates that they are fixed in the flexed position and are not naturally extended with the toes pointing down as would be the case if a person had just died from hanging.

But even if Fig. 9 were a depiction of a living person, and we concede that (1) the artist just forgot to draw a floor to stand on or (2) the person was consciously maintaining flexed feet (to say the least, an arduous task while hanging), we can only reach one conclusion: functionally, this person still is incapable of movement. The line of gravity entering the earth at his heels makes him flat footed and indicates a static posture from which it is very difficult to initiate movement. Moreover, both hips and knees are in a locked position, further inhibiting and limiting movement.

Fig. 10 represents the eastern concept of the optimal alignment of the human body and shows the centerline that the internal martial artist seeks to maintain. In most important ways it represents the complete antithesis of the model hanging in western medical offices. To begin with, note the different arrows on the line of gravity. The arrow on the western model is pointing down because it is established, passively, from the top down by the body hanging. The gravity line in the eastern model has arrowheads pointing both up and down, indicating that the body is striving to extend itself upward to counter the gravitational pull downward. Here the line of gravity is established actively in a standing position, rooting the body to the ground in such a way that it is ready to move in any direction at any moment.

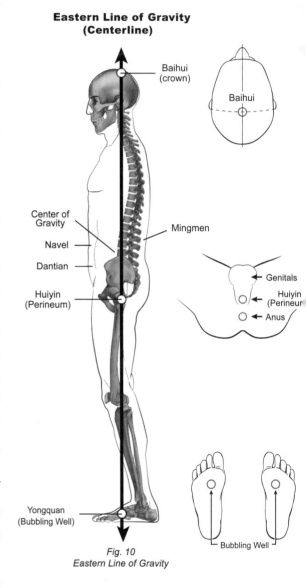

Fig. 10
Eastern Line of Gravity

In this eastern model, the alignment of the centerline is based on the principle of "three points on a line." The points are the three acupuncture points called the yong quan (bubbling well) in the feet, the hui yin point (perineum) between anus and genitals, and the baihui (百會) point at the crown of the head. When we examine the alignment of these three points from the ground up, we can see how it engages all the extensor muscles of the body, but particularly those of the legs and spine, to maximally extend the body vertically upward in space.

The line of gravity enters the ground towards the front of the feet at the yong quan, or bubbling well point, in the eastern model whereas in the western model, it enters the ground through the heels. Neurologically, the yong quan, or bubbling well point, is a reflex point that when stimulated, activates the extensor muscles of the legs into a readiness for posture and movement. Unlocking the knees, as shown, further facilitates this reflexive readiness. Here I invite the reader to perform a simple mind/body experiment to verify these observations. Simply stand with the feet parallel, close your eyes and in your mind picture yourself at the end of a diving board getting ready to jump off and dive. Notice that in preparing for the dive, you unlock, or even bend, the knees and shift your weight forward onto the balls of your feet.

Now let us consider the hui yin, or perineum, point between anus and genitals. It is not an easy thing to align the central gravity line to go through the perineum point. The main obstacles in this effort are chronically contracted musculature of the hips and lumbar spine, that have resulted in the average human being having largely frozen hips and pathological curvature of the spine. As will be described in detail in chapters that follow, the most important tool at our disposal to reverse this damage is the mindful use of the breath to loosen the frozen musculature and realign the posture. When the hips and spine loosen, the pelvis can be tilted and the tailbone pulled under and forward to position the perineum properly. The effect of this on the spine is to minimize the lumbar curve, effectively lengthening the spine. The resulting lower back feels flat, full, and above all, very strong, as it effectively integrates the lower and upper parts of the torso. The newly relaxed hips, moreover, allow us to reclaim the functional use and development of the torso's rotational abilities for martial arts and other uses.

At the top end of the spine it is much the same story as at the bottom end. Here a difference in conception of what constitutes the topmost point of the human body also gives rise to differences in the alignment of the centerline. The western model considers the top of the head to be the middle of the skull's flat, top surface, and hangs the body from that point. While this actually is the posture of the average person, it points to the pathology of the average: the excessive curvature of the cervical spine actually tilts the head back and tilts the chin more or less up, making the flat part of the head the "top." Effectively, this separates the head from the torso, and contributes to balance problems.

The eastern model aligns the top of the centerline at the baihui point at the very crown of the head. This point is several inches back from the top point in the western model. It only becomes the "top" of the head when the chin is dropped, in the process straightening the spine's cervical curvature, lengthening it upwards, and reintegrating the head with the torso, thus optimizing the whole body's central equilibrium.

To sum up, the western model of gravitational alignment is based on a body passively hanging from the head, immobile, whether dead or alive. The eastern model of proper gravitational alignment, on the other hand, is based on the body actively standing on its feet ready for action, i.e., movement. Let us now investigate this eastern model and its requirements in more detail.

Integrating Posture

I remember watching a documentary video on some of the old generation surfers of Hawaii, men and women in their 60s, 70s and 80s, still practicing and enjoying their beautiful and dangerous art in advanced age. In one segment, one of these pioneering masters was conducting a workshop to transmit the "secrets" of success to the younger generation. To the novice, the placement and movement of the feet seem of prime importance. But the old-school surfer stressed that the first thing in maintaining balance was to always keep the head up, so that the body can adjust underneath it. Olympic skiers and skaters offer a similar lesson: even as their bodies perform incredible acrobatics, their heads remain steady all the while.

The internal martial arts share with surfing and other sports an appreciation of the primacy of balance. In each, mastery requires great attention to the position of the head as the topmost part of our vertical structure, so that the body can be in balance and move freely underneath it. In standing meditation, because the position of the bottom-most part of our vertical structure, the feet, is equally important, we discuss both head and feet in the following paragraphs.

The importance of both feet and head in the maintenance of posture has been demonstrated clearly by modern science. Our overall sense of balance of the whole body is created as the cerebellum integrates two sub-conscious streams of neural information: the down-up stream that goes from feet to head, and the up-down stream that goes from head to feet. Standing meditation, right from the start, leads one to an awareness and integration of these two subconscious phenomena.

Accordingly, the first two instructions to the new student of standing meditation pertain to the feet and the head. After the instructions for bottom (feet) and top (head), we will examine how the remaining middle segments of the body are integrated around its vertical axis into the state of central equilibrium. Needless to say, though the discussion here is necessarily linear and sequential, ultimately the awareness it seeks to cultivate is simultaneous.

In standing meditation, the feet are placed parallel to each other, shoulder width apart for men, and hip width apart for women. The toes should be turned in a few degrees so that the outsides of the feet are parallel. The knees are unlocked but not bent. The difference is important -one has the same height whether the knees are locked or unlocked, but when the knees are bent, one's height will be lower. The weight of the body enters the ground on what the Chinese call the yongquan, or bubbling well points of each foot.

The bubbling well point is located just behind the ball of the foot. In traditional Chinese medicine, this is a critical energy gate and acupuncture point. In western medicine, it is an important reflex point that when stimulated, activates the extensors of the leg.[9] Consciously placing the majority of the weight over these points helps to activate/ stimulate the reflex, which we can experience as awareness of the springiness of the legs pushing our torso up. As mentioned previously, the feeling is as if we are ready to jump up, like the diver at the end of the board preparing for a dive.

By making the bubbling well points act as the center of each foot, we can distribute the weight evenly around the periphery of both feet. Paying attention to equal weight distribution between the inside and the outside of the feet, as well as the

---

[9] Deane Juhan, op. cit., p.172.

front and the back, will train the pressure-sensing nerve endings located throughout the surface of the feet. As a result, these nerve endings will give us increasingly accurate feedback regarding any deviation from optimal weight distribution.

The knees are critically important in stabilizing the feet. To get the right feeling, one should imagine holding a balloon between the knees. Then imagine filling this balloon with air and feel the expansion putting the weight on the outside of the feet. Then, keeping the knees where they are, shift the weight back toward the inside of the feet until it is distributed 50/50 inside and outside. This provides the proper oppositional tension for the most stable base.

At the same time, maintain two-thirds of the weight on the bubbling well and one-third on the heel. This stabilizes vertical structure by minimizing both the unintended forward/backward tilting, as well as the lateral shifting from foot to foot, of the center of gravity line. Moreover, imagining the ball between the knees not only stabilizes and integrates the feet and lower leg, but also enables the integration of the entire leg with the lower torso by means of the hip joints.

In standing meditation the head is held high, as if trying to touch the sky with the crown of the skull, or as if balancing a jug of water on it. The slight pushing up with the crown actually allows the neck muscles to relax, causing the chin to drop a little and the eyes to look forward horizontally so that they naturally gaze at the horizon. As we have seen, tucking the chin in lightly straightens the cervical curve and makes the crown, or more precisely, the baihui acupuncture point, the top of the head. It's important to reiterate that this alignment differs from the western notion that the flat part of the skull is the top of the head, a notion that derives from widespread, habitual, and excessive cervical curvature.

The correct postural positioning of the head not only minimizes the cervical curvature, but produces a sensation that the torso is hanging from the head. This stretching, elongating and relaxing the neck is the objective, rather than the feeling that the head is resting as a dead weight on the body. Because the joint receptors around the vertebrae in the neck provide the balance organs in the inner ear with information pertaining to the position and movement of the torso, a relaxed neck is critically important in optimizing the sense of balance. If the head leans one way or another habitually, it impedes the optimal flow of balance and positional information to the central nervous system in two ways. One, some muscles are too tight and others too lax, and both impair the flow of neural data streams. Second, because the head weighs a lot the body wants to fall the way the head leans, and is prevented from doing so only by unconscious muscular exertion employed to counteract it. In other words, if the head is out of true vertical and horizontal alignment, the chances of losing balance increase significantly.

The number of neural calculations and instructions by the central nervous system necessary to maintain body balance multiply geometrically when the head is moving or positioned off the optimal horizontal and vertical planes. The more these neural demands increase, the more difficult it will be to maintain the balance and posture of the body. Since the organs of balance — the inner ears and the eyes — are situated in the head, cultivating optimal position of the head is critical to making the unconscious balance reflexes conscious. It is for this reason that standing meditation trains us to keep the head as still and stable as possible in order to facilitate and hone the overall postural stability and balance of our entire body.

Just as standing meditation instructions tell us to straighten out the cervical spinal curve, they also tell us to straighten the lumbar spinal curve. The essential technique in the straightening of the lumbar curve is to use the pelvic tilt to point the coxyx, or tail bone, towards the ground, as opposed to its normal tendency to curve backward. Think of tucking the tail between the legs, or of sitting down on a high bar stool. Skeletally and structurally, toeing in a bit, unlocking the knees and holding the ball between them, facilitates this pelvic tilt, and correctly positions the legs' femurs in the hip sockets.

The pelvic tilt and straightening of the lumbar curve is the primary structural requirement for the integration of the lower with the upper torso, and for making the power of the former accessible to the latter. We maintain this integration of the lower torso by a slight contraction of the iliopsoas group of hip flexor muscles. In the internal martial arts tradition, pushing out the lumbar spine and minimizing its curve is called opening the "gate of life" or "filling the ming men." Under normal circumstances the action of the iliopsoas group in producing the pelvic tilt is helped by the contraction of the rectus abdominis, the large muscle group in the front of the body that connects the rib cage to the pelvis and pubic bones. But when the pelvis is tilted in the standing meditation postures, the rectus abdominis must remain completely relaxed, i.e., the belly is not tense and pulled in, but allowed to hang naturally.

I often demonstrate this integrative effect to students in the following way. I will stand normally, with a pronounced lumbar curve, and ask one of them to push me gently

in the small of the back at the junction the third and fourth lumbar vertebrae. Because the upper and lower torsos are effectively disintegrated under this condition, a student finds that very little pressure can easily cause me to lose my balance. Then I repeat the same instruction but I move into my meditative stance and have the same student feel how I straighten out the lumber curve. I ask the student to push me again with the same amount of force as before. Now it is very easy to withstand quite a strong force applied at the same spot, making a persuasive demonstration of increased stability.

Fig. 11
Basic Standing
Meditation Posture

The default posture in standing meditation (Fig. 11) is known as the universal posture, or post. We hold the two arms in front of the body anywhere between the abdomen and the eyes. Usually, however, we hold the arms at shoulder level. This strengthens the upper back through stretching its muscles, and at the same time allows the chest to relax. Here, working with the image of embracing or holding a ball can be effective in eliciting the proper sensation, namely, that the hands, forearms, upper arms, shoulders and upper back constitute a structural, functional and energetic circle. Holding our elbows in front and slightly to the side of the body, we keep them bent at just over 90 degrees. The wrists and fingers slightly curve and open also as if each hand is holding a ball. The palms line up with the shoulders. All this is in accordance with the instructions from the internal martial arts classics, such as Yang Chengfu's (楊澄甫) "Ten Points"[10] and Wang Xiangzhai's "The Right Path of Yiquan"[11].

[10] Yang Cheng Fu, "*The Ten Essentials of Taijiquan Theory*" in "*Mastering Yang Style Taijiquan*" by Fu Zhongwen, Louis Swaim, transl., North Atlantic Books, Berkeley, CA, pp 16-19.

[11] Wang Xiangzhai, "*The Right Path of Yiquan*", Timo Heikkila & Li Jong, transl., ebook, 2001, pp. 7-8.

Natural and Normal Breathing

When a person sets off on the path of internal martial arts body/mind transformation, she must be very clear on the distinction between natural and normal breathing patterns. Natural breathing is what we're born with; normal breathing is what most individuals grow into with age. Natural breathing is healthy and powers one's life energy; normal breathing is unhealthy (both deteriorative and pathological) and drains one's life energy. Consequently, the first phase of the transformative process consists precisley of reversing the damage already done and transforming his "normal breathing" back into "natural breathing," as the very foundation of good health.

We were born breathing naturally, so it is to the newborn that we must look for the defining characteristics of natural breathing. Watch a baby when resting or sleeping to observe the rhythm of its breath. As the baby inhales, its tummy and rib cage inflate, or expand; on the exhalation, the tummy and rib cage deflate. From the outside, it seems a simple and straightforward rhythm. But to produce this fundamental rhythm, internally a complex choreography must take place. The diaphragm, the muscles of the pleural and abdominal cavities, and the spine, all interact cooperatively in the breathing process.

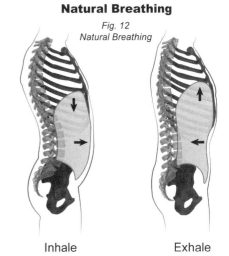

Natural Breathing

Fig. 12
Natural Breathing

Inhale   Exhale

The muscles most directly involved in the expansion of the chest during the inhale are the diaphragm and the intercostal muscles surrounding the rib cage. The major partner is the diaphragm, which accounts for 75 percent of the effort, while the intercostal chest muscles contribute 25 percent. When the diaphragm contracts, the chest cavity is enlarged and the inhale occurs as air is actively sucked into the lungs.

Moreover, as the diaphragm contracts, it pushes down on the contents of the abdominal cavity. To accommodate this displacement of abdominal viscera during contraction of the diaphragm, the abdominal muscles relax and the tummy inflates (Fig. 12). In other words, the abdominal musculature–particularly the transverse abdominus–and the diaphragm work in opposite but complimentary ways.

On the exhale the exact opposite occurs. As the diaphragm relaxes, the chest cavity deflates and pushes the air up out of the lungs. The abdomen also deflates as the muscles of the abdominal wall contract (Fig. 12), elevating the dome of the diaphragm and helping to evacuate the used air.

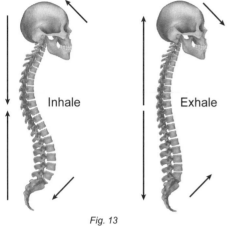

Fig. 13
Spinal Mechanics and the Breath

In a truly flexible spine such as that possessed by the very young, the spine also participates in the breathing process with a characteristic undulation. In natural breathing, on the inhale, the top and bottom tips of the spine (head and tail) will tend to bend back, maximize their curvatures, and arch the spine (Fig. 13). On the exhale, again, the reverse happens. The top and bottom tips of the spine tend to bend forward, minimizing the spinal curves and straightening the spine (Fig. 13). To sum up, the main characteristic of the natural breathing pattern is the complete participation and integration of the various body parts and systems, including the diaphragm, the abdominal muscles, the rib cage and the muscles of the chest, and the spine and its associated musculature.

...

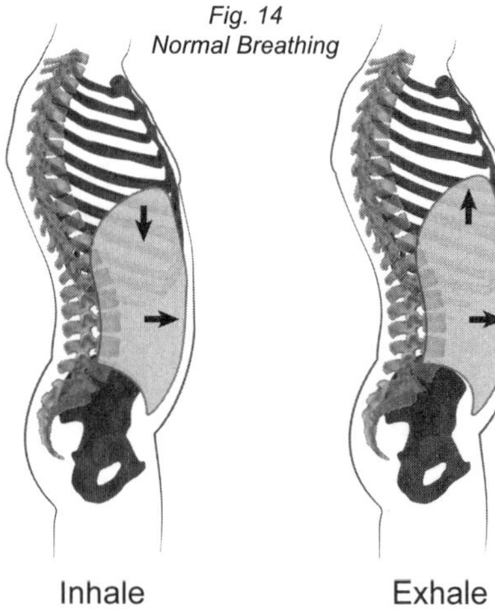

The sad story of many if not most human lives is that people start out breathing naturally, i.e., optimally as babies, but deteriorate into adulthood patterns where what is normal is no longer natural. Breathing and postural patterns become affected for the worse, diminished by the stresses and strains of modern life. In the average adult, normal breathing is characterized by a diminution of all interrelated norms of form and function. Chronically contracted, the diaphragm itself is diminished in vigor and

Normal Breathing

Fig. 14
Normal Breathing

Inhale   Exhale

capacity. The abdominal muscles are frequently so weakened they can no longer participate (Fig. 14) and the chest muscles often are so tight they do not allow the proper expansion of the rib cage. Likewise, the spinal curves have become so frozen that the spine for all intents and purposes has become immobilized and has lost its ability to participate in the breathing process.

The contracted, frozen diaphragm and associated musculature of the normal breathing pattern results in a pattern of shallow breathing centered solely in the chest. Over the long term, this results in a chronically frozen posture of inhalation that is symptomatic of the pathology of the normal breathing pattern. The chest appears pushed out permanently, the shoulders are pulled back in a chronic state of contraction, and the abdominal muscles are chronically over-stretched by the abdominal contents. It is as though the body is always gasping for air and never getting enough. The pathology of the normal breathing pattern is twin to, and mirrored by, the pathology of the normal spine. The spine exhibits permamently immobilized curvatures of the lumbar and cervical segments typical of the posture of inhalation (Fig. 13). Frozen, the spine neither participates in the inhale nor the exhale. The result is a functional segmentation of upper and lower parts of the spine and torso.

Standing meditation emphasizes the posture and mechanics of natural exhalation in the postural realignment of the body's parts. Why? When we are startled by something, we hold our breath. When the situation passes, we may let out a sigh in relief. In other words, inhalation is the phase of the breath associated with holding tension in the body and exhalation is the phase of the breath associated with the release of tension. Ergo, if you want to release long held chronic tensions that adversely affect your posture and movement, you will have to engage in a sustained and systematic practise of "relearning" how to exhale.

Generally, in both the natural breathing of the baby and the normal breathing of the adult, the exhalation is entirely passive because it happens when the diaphragm relaxes. By making the exhalation active rather than passive, standing meditation restores diaphragmatic function and spinal mobility. Specifically, the conscious use of the pelvic tilt and contraction of the abdominal muscles simultaneous with a lengthened exhale will result, in time, in the gradual unfreezing of the diaphragm. This will restore natural breathing ability, remobilize the lumbar spine and restore the functional integration of the lower and upper parts of the trunk in posture, breath and movement.

Just as the bodily functions of posture and breath become dissociated from each other and deteriorate in function, so the body as a whole becomes dissociated from the mind. And with the deterioration of posture and breath, there is a corresponding deterioration in the mental faculties that should control them. This creates negative feedback loops between the somatic functions and the mental faculties, which tend to spiral out of control unless conscious steps are taken to halt and reverse the process.

The Chinese internal health and martial arts promise a state of glowing health through the diligent practice of posture, breath and mind. Standing meditation is a kind of therapy in which mindfulness transforms normal breathing and posture back into natural breathing and posture. To find our way back to what is natural, as opposed to normal, we must follow the advice Lao Tse gave over two thousand years ago: "… divest yourself from what you acquired after birth and return to find your original self … [to] control the vital force to achieve gentleness and become like the newborn child."[12]

Integrating Awareness

Awareness of our internal environment comes from the internal senses of central equilibrium and proprioception. Awareness of our external environment comes from our external senses: visual, auditory, olfactory and tactile. Ultimately, because of its stillness, standing meditation is the easiest method for cultivating the simultaneous awareness of both our internal and external environments. The next challenge is to maintain this awareness while moving. The highest, most difficult level requires maintaining this awareness while physically interacting with a training partner or opponent.

To achieve this holistic awareness, the first and foremost requirement is that we must stop thinking and/or daydreaming and start cultivating awareness of each of our individual senses. Then, in each of the senses, the expansion of awareness requires a shift from hard to soft focus—literally, a shift in perspective from the center of perception to the periphery, from foreground to background. This allows us to come to experience awareness as the simultaneity of perceptions in time and space.

---

[12] Lin Yu Tang, ed., *"The Wisdom Of Laotse,"* Random House, New York, 1948, p. 83.

Externally, take vision as an example. Standing meditation instructs us to (soft) focus our eyes in the distance in order to activate our peripheral vision, because focused vision excludes perception of anything but the focused-on object, and leads to a linearity of time and experience. Focused perception makes a temporal sequence out of simultaneous object/events. For example, when I use focused vision and shift my focus from object to object, I am creating a linear sequence of perception (and therefore of time) from what is, in fact, simultaneous. But when I look at something far away in the distance, my peripheral visual sense will kick in to widen my field of perception. I can perceive all of these objects simultaneously in my peripheral vision. In the primeval sense of the alerting mechanism, using soft focus enables "field awareness" by allowing one to detect any movement in the wider field of vision.

The external senses of hearing and smell can also have a hard or a soft focus, and the more we meditate, the more these perceptions will be based on soft rather than hard focus. For example, if we focus our ears on one sound in the environment, dominant though it may be, we don't hear all the other sounds that constitute the background. Opening up our ears to the sea of background noise, we increase our awareness of all things going on in our environment.

Likewise in the sense of touch, we can distinguish between hard and soft focus. Often we are unaware of the tactile sensory dimension, or we only pay attention when some stronger or more intense sensation demands our attention. The more we meditate, the more the sense of touch opens up into soft focus and we become more simultaneously aware of the sensory input upon our entire skin. In this way, the skin surface becomes the periphery of our being. As Wang Xiangzhai describes this sensitizing process, it entails the hairs on the arms and the rest of the body standing straight like halberds (mao fa ru ji: 毛發如戟)[13], just as our animal cousins raise their hackles when facing danger.

---

[13] Wang Xiangzhai, "*The Essence of Martial Art: The Theory of Yiquan*," translated by Liu Jong, ebook, 2001, p. 323.

Soft-focusing of the attention also applies to the internal senses, especially the sense of balance. Internally, the relaxed awareness of central equilibrium entails a soft focus on the center point of the centerline. This, of course, is our very center of gravity in the abdomen. While being softly focused there, we hold both ends of the spine-tail and head- in awareness at the same time. Consistent practice with soft focus on the abdominal center allows for ever widening and deepening inner perception of postural and motor processes, and ultimately, the experience of ji rou ruo yi (肌肉若一)[14], meaning "the muscles as one."

Standing meditation leads us to an awareness of the three spatial polarities consisting of the six directions (up-down, front-back, left-right) emanating from the abdominal center of gravity. We must work at developing awareness of each of these six directions separately and sequentially. As the awareness expands, we become simultaneously aware of both poles of each pair and finally of the three spatial polarities, that is, all six directions, simultaneously. In this way we begin to experience the stillness of standing mediation, not as absence of movement due to muscular inactivity, but as a dynamic stillness that is pregnant with movement in all directions, each movement only being held in check by a movement in the opposite direction.

Developing simultaneous awareness of all six directions emanating from our abdominal center of gravity, we begin to experience increasing degrees of roundness and the sense of our being as a sphere. First there is the roundness of the center, as the abdomen itself relaxes, fills with qi, and takes on a balloon-like feeling. Secondly, there is the roundness of the arms which are holding a ball. And thirdly, with the unlocked knees holding the balloon between them combining with the springiness from the bottom of the feet, there is even a roundness about the foundation. All three of these balls start to merge and in time we begin to experience them as one sphere. Let us examine more closely the unique characteristics of that sphere.

---

[14] Ibid.

Three Dimensions, Six Directions

In discussing balance and movement, I often ask my students to perform the following thought experiment. *Imagine you're camping in the mountains and somehow you lost time getting back to your campground. It's dark now and you've lost your flashlight. Plus, in addition to the very steep ravine on the side, the path down to your campground is very narrow, with a lot of rocks on it and holes in it. The question is: "How do you walk?"* Invariably, the students answer correctly: *"Very carefully."* When pressed to illustrate what that means, they will put their weight on one foot and explore the ground in front of them with the other, sensing obstacles and not putting any weight on the

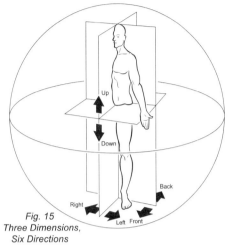

Fig. 15
Three Dimensions,
Six Directions

second foot until it has found a patch of ground that feels safe. This is mindfulness in walking and movement, and in the internal martial arts, it is this kind of awareness and stability that we are cultivating, whether in simple solo walking, doing the taijiquan form, or in partnered practice.

Meditation is mindfulness, and moving meditation is therefore also a form of mindfulness, a paying attention to and becoming aware of how we move in space. The characteristics of our upright bipedal posture determine how exactly we can move in the three-dimensional, six-directional space that emanates from our center of gravity. By virtue of the functional division of labor among the parts of our upright posture, it is the top (head-mind) that directs the bottom (legs) to move the center (abdomen) along the three axes of our personal space: the vertical axis, the horizontal axis and the rotational axis (Fig. 15).

It is the job of the legs, our foundation, to move our torso in space. The three leg joints each specialize in allowing movement in one dimension, while playing a supporting role in movement in the other two. In the movement of the torso, the knees are the critical joints that allow both vertical and horizontal movement of the frame. When flexed-extended simultaneously, the knees allow vertical up-down movement of the torso; while when flexed-extended alternately, they allow for horizontal movement. The ankles allow the torso to make the fine adjustments required to remain plumb during both horizontal and vertical movement. The hip joints allow movement of the upright body in the horizontal left-right dimension by rotating the torso around the centerline axis either clockwise (right) or counterclockwise (left).

...

Vertical movement of the centerline in parallel or archer stance is accomplished by alternately bending and straightening both knees slowly. This action lowers and raises the centerline and allows the lower torso, upper torso and head to move as a unit (Fig. 16). The internal lengthening of the spine along the centerline which standing meditation practice prescribes, must be maintained while moving up-down along the vertical axis.

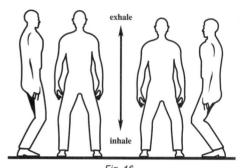

Fig. 16
Vertical Movement of the Centerline

Because it is less important to have a large range of movement than to be able to use and control whatever range of movement we do have, extending that range is a secondary objective. The primary objective is to begin moving correctly within the range our joints allow, with full attention to all the demanding postural details we described in the previous chapter. The most common postural mistakes include sticking the butt out backwards, and/or the chest forward, inclining the head forward or backward, and leaning the torso forward, backward, or sideways.

What's the objective of these prescriptions? Central equilibrium! This is the secret weapon of the internal martial arts. To the extent that the practitioner inclines his body, or any part of it, in either stillness or movement, he will be unable to learn and execute either the offensive skills (fajin) or the defensive skills (listening and following) of the internal martial arts.

In order to keep the spine extended maximally during its vertical movement, cultivate this awareness: while lowering the trunk and center of gravity by flexing the legs, feel as if the head is resisting, ever so lightly, the downward movement of the tail. Conversely, while raising the trunk by means of extension of the legs, the head must lead and the tail must follow.

...

Walking is essentially moving the (vertical) centerline along the horizontal axis. In normal, everyday stepping and walking, we initiate forward movement by unconsciously leaning the torso forward a bit and then picking up a foot in order to place it out in front to prevent a fall. Thus normal walking is a perpetual falling with a perpetual self-recovery. In the internal martial arts, however, losing control of balance and movement is highly dangerous, and so we must unlearn this walking-by-falling method of locomotion.

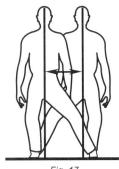

Fig. 17
Horizontal Movement
of the Centerline

Shifting in the horizontal plane (Fig. 17) is a critical movement skill. It is used offensively in delivering the force (fajin) and defensively in following, yielding and sticking. Therefore, this is another focus for mindful movement meditation – the shifting of the torso in the horizontal plane from foot to foot while maintaining absolute perpendicularity of the centerline, neither leaning it forward nor backward. A simple practice exercise is this: in the archer stance, shift back and forth slowly by alternately extending the leg that's bent while flexing the leg that's extended.

Walking is shifting the centerline followed by stepping; that is, we lift and place the un-weighted foot to the front or rear, and then alternate and repeat the process. Indeed, stepping is a moving meditation in itself. Standing with all the weight on one leg, mindfully pick up the other leg and place it alternately in the front, back, left, right - basically, in any direction. The requirement is simple, but not that easy: keep the body absolutely still and in balance.

The dangers of leaning the torso either forward or backward are even greater in stepping and walking than in mere shifting. Therefore, be mindful that regardless of whether the foot that is being placed touches the ground first with the heel, toe, or both simultaneously, it must establish secure contact with the ground before the other foot initiates the weight-shifting process. Moving too soon causes leaning, and even falling.

After some practice moving the center in the horizontal plane, when the movement has become smooth and even, we start to develop the sensation that our center, much like a ball or a wheel, is rolling forward, and that the distance of the center to the ground never varies. Oliver Wendell Holmes observed more than a century ago:

> Man is a *wheel* with two spokes, his legs, and two fragments of a tire, his feet. He rolls successively on each of these fragments from the heel to the toe. If he had spokes enough, he would go round and round as the boys do when they "make a wheel" with their four limbs for its spokes. But having only two available for ordinary locomotion, each of these has to be taken up as soon as it's used, and carry forward to be used again, and so alternately with the pair.[15]
>
> ...

Finally, our upright bipedal posture gives human beings the unique ability to rotate our trunk clockwise or counterclockwise (right or left) around the centerline axis (Fig. 18). Whether in parallel or archer stance, one must be mindful to keep the ball between the knees to stabilize the legs' structure, and then slowly to practice rotating the trunk clockwise and counterclockwise. The main rule here is that there must be no twisting of the spine, which occurs when the shoulders move independently of the hips. Instead, the upper and lower trunk must be unified in the effort, so that the hips and shoulder at all times remain in alignment.

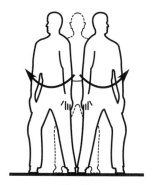

Fig. 18
Rotational Movement
of the Centerline

Becoming a Sphere

Yang Chengfu wrote that "the human body is like a sphere and the limbs and bones are all laid out along curves."[16] Let us further explore this sphericality of the body

[15] Mabel Ellsworth Todd, "The Thinking Body," New York: Dance Horizons, 1972, p. 195.

[16] Yang Chengfu, the Brennan translation, op.cit.

he describes. We have observed that in standing meditation, the lower part (legs), the center part (abdomen) and the upper part (the arms) each feel as if holding a ball. Gradually these combine into an overall sensation of spherical awareness and the body as a whole begins to feel more and more like a big ball. We've also seen how it is the function of the lower portion of that sphere, the legs, to move the sphere's center. The function of the upper portion of the sphere, on the other hand, is to allow us to change the shape of the sphere, by means of movement of the arms, without changing or losing the internal sensation of the integrated body.

The position of the arms and hands in the universal post posture is the "middle-way" and the nexus or point of intersection of four polarities: up-down, out-in to the front; open-close to the sides; and clockwise or counterclockwise rotation. Exploring the parameters and structure of our sphere in our movement meditation, it is best to begin very simply by exploring each polarity. For example, along the vertical axis, we can simply move both arms simultaneously from their lowest to their highest positions and back. Next we can explore the front-back axis by extending and retracting the arms, then the left-right axis by opening and closing the arms.

As these basic movements define the spatial parameters of our sphere, the potential of movement within this sphere becomes near infinite in its variety due to several other characteristics. These include the ability of the arms, particularly the forearms, to rotate along their longitudinal axis[17], the ability of the simple movements to combine into complex patterns, and the ability of the two arms to engage in different movements.

Due to the versatility of the human arms, it is possible to generate innumerable arm postures. These postures can give an infinite variety of shapes to our sphere, each for a specific purpose, yet all the while the sphere maintains its integrity, i.e., its central equilibrium and its internal structure.

Moreover, when all the possible combinations of the arm positions are multiplied by all the possible torso positions along its vertical, horizontal and rotational axes, the possibilities for generating movement further increases exponentially.[18]

---

[17] My friend and student Greg Pass has pointed out to me that the rotational ability of the arms imparts a mobius strip like geometry to the human sphere, in as much as a simple rotation can change the point of contact, without moving it, from the outside to the inside and visa versa. Greg Pass, Personal Communication, 5/22/2012.

[18] A more detailed discussion of this can be found in my two previous books: "*Qigong of the Center: Essence of Taijiquan*" and "*The Tao of Yiquan: The Method of Awareness in the Martial Arts,*" Qi Works, Walnut Creek, CA.

All the principles and techniques of the internal martial arts are incorporated in their forms. "Everything is in the form," Master Tam never tires of reiterating. And indeed the internal martial arts forms were created as repositories, or libraries, of ancient, deep knowledge of the complete fundamentals of posture and movement. Practically speaking, movement in the internal martial arts is a transition from one posture to another posture. Forms are defined sequences of specialized postures that have at least one, but usually several, applications for use in attack or defense. Forms teach us to move the center in any direction and to change the shape of our sphere at will, while maintaining its internal integrity.

The dialectic of movement and stillness is closely intertwined with the dialectic of offense and defense. Because internal martial arts strategy and philosophy is to let the opponent make the first move to attack, movement is used primarily for defense. The purpose of "following" and "yielding" are embodied in the transitions between the postures of the form, and their purpose is to capture the opponent's center while moving to a better position to attack. Once the opponent's center has been captured, movement can be stopped anytime. The result is a posture, the stillness of which is then used for its primary offensive function: the issuance of jin.

Movement in the internal martial arts forms is based on the principle of the circle. The circle is the embodiment of the yielding principle that entails: (1) accepting and going along with an incoming hostile energy, and then (2) taking control over it and (3) redirecting it back towards the source.

In the internal martial arts forms, the three movements of the centerline combine to produce the two primary circular patterns: the horizontal and the vertical circle. The horizontal circle is accomplished through the shifting and/or rotational movements of the centerline, while the vertical circle is accomplished through a combination of horizontal and vertical movements of the centerline. Naturally they can be combined to make an infinite numbers of diagonal circles.

Doing our forms with awareness of the circles they contain helps us to consolidate our experience of ourselves as spherical beings. As will be developed further in Part 2, the pulsing movements of the center and the circling movements of the arms functionally resemble the structure of a cell, with the center of gravity in the abdomen as the inner nucleus and the range of arm movements constituting the outer perimeter of it's tactile reach.

...

So far in our investigations, we have gone from stillness to movement and now it is time to close the circle and go back to stillness. As the taiji classics put it, since all movement (taiji) comes from stillness (wuji 無極), so all movement (taiji) must also return to stillness (wuji).

All movements, simple or complex, can range in their expression from very large to very small. In the internal martial arts terminology, the three main practice methods are often referred as "big frame," "medium frame," and "small frame" forms. The medium frame is utilized generally in learning and teaching the forms. Movements neither large nor small, but in between, lend themselves best to the teaching/learning environment. Once learned, the movements of the forms can be made larger for purposes of stretching and strengthening. This is "big frame" practice.

The more advanced levels of practice utilize the "small frame" forms to prepare one for their application in playing or fighting. Why? Because, as Master Yang Chengfu wrote, "… the area in which taiji techniques operate is maybe the width of a hair and widens to perhaps no bigger than an inch, and so there is not much of a window for miscalculation. If you are wrong by a hair, you might as well be a thousand miles away."[19] Master Wang Xiangzhai expressed the same idea when he said: "Small movement is better than big movement; no movement is better than small movement." To go back from movement to stillness in such a way that the new stillness remains charged with the potential for new movement, in any direction, one must both understand and practice the procedure called the "internalization of movement."

---

[19] Yang Chengfu, the Brennan translation, op.cit.

To get the concept, do a simple movement, say, shifting back and forth from front to back foot, a number of times, and each successive time you do it, make the movement a little smaller, gradually making the movements so small that there is no longer any visible external movement. Yet on the inside you continue to have the sensation of the back and forth shifting movement. Then stop the alternating pulses and just be still but ready to move in either direction. Thoroughly practice all fundamental movements this way until, when still, you are ready to move in any direction. Then begin to do the same procedure with more complex movements and eventually, even an entire form sequence.

One internalizes circular movement by making the circles of movement smaller and smaller until no external movement is visible. The body moving in circles becomes circles moving in the body and the energy of the body's movement becomes the movement of energy throughout the body. Standing meditation infused with this type of ready stillness, increases the responsiveness of our motor system to external and internal stimuli. Ultimately, the responsive circle of defense and offense can be made internally and so small that it is both instantaneous and imperceptible, resulting in the attacker being bounced back the moment she makes contact.

When moving in circles becomes second nature to us, we begin to experience our bodies more and more as being spherical. For after all, in conditions of gravity, the parameters of a sphere may be described as one vertical circle, one horizontal circle, and an infinite number of diagonal circles around a common center. As we will investigate in detail in Part 2, that common center of gravity is in our abdomen, in what the Chinese tradition calls the dantian area. As our circular movements begin to revolve in three dimensions of space around the dantian, our internal perception of our bodies becomes ever more spherical.

Chapter 3: Making the Involuntary Voluntary

There are involuntary types of stillness and movement, and there are voluntary types of stillness and movement. Involuntary stillness and movement often occur in crisis situations and are triggered by sub-cortical neural impulses, both simple reflexes based in the spine and more complex fixed action patterns, or faps – the learned behavior patterns that reside in the basal ganglia of the mid-brain. These reflexes include the balance reflex, the startle reflex, the stretch and tendon reflexes, the opposition and collapsing reflexes, the flight and fight reflexes, the tensing reflex, the whole body reflex, and the breathing reflex.

These reflexes are hard-wired by evolution in adaptations in the human brain and central nervous system. But, when we are startled or when we tense, when we are provoked to fight-or-flight alert, these reflexes limit our response to challenges and create vulnerabilities that can be exploited by an opponent. The stillness and movement meditations of the internal martial arts are designed to de-activate these involuntary responses and make them voluntary. More specifically, the training has twin objectives: to eliminate all involuntary reflexes and faps through superior awareness, and to learn to induce these reflexes in our opponents.

In essence, the internal martial arts cultivate awareness and control over postural and balance reflexes and thereby enhance our equilibrium, relaxation and integration at a fundamental level. At the same time, this training is essential to developing the offensive and defensive skills of the internal martial arts. Through internal martial arts training, we learn to induce a loss of control in the opponent that creates a window of opportunity for our successful attack.

Startle or Freeze Reflex

The antelope is peacefully grazing on the savannah. Across the plain, birds screech suddenly and lift off in alarm. Startled, the antelope stops its munching and freezes, then raises its head to scan its surroundings, trying to locate and identify the danger.

Fig. 19
Where the Tiger
and the Antelope Roam

Almost simultaneously, it readies itself to bolt and get away by lowering itself on its haunches. On the other side of the plain the tiger is lazily ambling along through the grasses. All of a sudden it glimpses the antelope through an opening in the bush. It stops all its movement, raises its head to pinpoint the prey and assess its chances for a successful pursuit, and gets ready and sinks into a crouch (Fig. 19). Whether predator or prey, when unexpected events interrupt an activity, the startle reflex in both operates the same way. The startle reflex is the hardwired mechanism that pushes the reset button and reorients the entire sensory-motor system for an immediate change in behavior.

As such, the startle reflex, also called the "freeze reflex," has sensory and motor components. These are the alerting and crouch reflexes, respectively, that occur at opposite ends of the spine. At the top of the spine, the alerting reflex consists of lengthening the cervical curve by lifting or raising the head ("cocking" or "craning") to mobilize the total perceptual apparatus of eyes, ears and nose. At the tail end, the crouch reflex lengthens the spine by eliminating the lumbar curve. It also mobilizes the deep muscles of the trunk and legs to be ready for flight or fight.

When we recall the postural instructions of the internal martial arts, we can see that standing meditation and the startle reflex have deep commonalities in structure and function. Structurally, when the classics instruct us "sink the qi and raise the spirit," they also direct us to position the tailbone in order to minimize the curvature of the lumbar spine and position the head to minimize the cervical curvature. Functionally, they share a "ready for anything" stillness that allows a heightened awareness of the environment, as well as a complete mobilization of the motor system to enable instantaneous response to any changes in the external environment. In the words of Master Yang Chengfu, the postural "energy in Taiji of containing the chest and pulling up your back...is the attitude of a cat pouncing on a mouse... (it is) waiting for the opportunity and then issuing."[20]

---

[20] Yang Chengfu, the Brennan translation, op.cit.

And yet, this similarity should not suggest the startle reflex and the state of standing meditation are identical. Rather, it is as if standing meditation has simply isolated and adapted the acute awareness that comes with the startle reflex. By cultivating greater perceptual awareness, standing meditation seeks to eliminate, or at least minimize, the many negative effects that come with the startle reflex.

The startle reflex achieves sensory motor integration for readiness by means of involuntary tension. The sympathetic nervous stimulation and adrenal pituitary hormonal secretions affect the body in profound ways. Brain and body produce more adrenalin and other crisis hormones. The heart beats faster and the breathing speeds up; blood pressure jumps. Less blood flows to the periphery of the body, but more flows to the core. The body creates physical integration through muscular contraction as it readies for action.

As a readiness practice, standing meditation transforms and transcends this crisis response as the best method to achieve sensory-motor integration and readiness. Through alert and voluntary relaxation, standing mediation stimulates the parasympathetic nervous system. Because the parasympathetic nervous system governs the restorative functions when the body is at rest, the physiological effects of standing meditation are completely the opposite of the startle reflex: the heart rate falls, blood flows from the core to the periphery, and a flood of hormones produces a sense of well-being and pleasure.

We have seen how relaxation practice in standing meditation creates a "ready to go" state of being by realigning of the skeletal bones embedded in the web of the muscles and connective tissue into a finely tuned, but relaxed, structure. In like manner, standing meditation brings our senses into a state of relaxation, leading to habits of soft-focus and simultaneity of perception in each individual sense. Over time, we achieve the ability to maintain soft-focus and experience the simultaneity of all internal and external sensory perception. The visual, auditory, olfactory and tactile sense awarenesses combine with the sense awareness of equilibrium and kinesthesia into a single whole awareness of the relationship between organism and environment. In this way, we neutralize and transcend the startle reflex.

The voluntary stillness of standing meditation prevents the involuntary stillness of the startle reflex. Why is this important? Obviously, for general health reasons, it's beneficial to startle less frequently because startle activates our crisis physiology. In the internal martial arts it can even be a matter of life and death: one of the internal martial artist's essential techniques is eliciting the startle reflex in the opponent. This skill can be said to be one of the internal martial artist's "secret" weapons. For the moment that the involuntary stiffening of the startle reflex occurs constitutes a moment of extreme vulnerability and danger.

Balance Reflex

As we've already examined in detail, the efficient control of posture is important both during standing and during walking. Stable posture is necessary to provide support for voluntary limb, head or trunk movements. Maintenance of postural stability is mostly a non-volitional activity based, to a large extent, on in-born neural mechanisms that use proprioceptive feedback information. The complex mechanism by which we automatically correct our body position when we begin to lose our equilibrium is called the balance or "righting" reflex.

For the martial artist, being and staying in balance is even more critical. Loss of balance means loss of control, and loss of control means vulnerability to attack; loss of balance is, in fact, a matter of life and death. Therefore, in the central equilibrium training of the standing and moving meditations of the internal martial arts, we become aware of our involuntary postural and movement habits. Awareness alone allows us to gain control over involuntary movement and loss of balance. All movement becomes voluntary and balance is never lost.

Awareness of balance and then control over balance begins with one's self, and eventually extends to one's opponent. Like the startle reflex, the loss-of-balance reflex causes the involuntary tensing of the body. Therefore, the internal martial artist has inter-related goals. First, it is to never lose balance, for without central equilibrium, one cannot master either the offensive skill of fajin (energy discharge) or defensive skills of yielding and sticking. No less important, the internal martial artist seeks to induce the loss of balance in his opponent so that the paralysis of involuntary tension makes the opponent vulnerable to attack.

Whole Body Reflex

The diaphragm is one of the most central and powerful muscles in the body. It literally divides the torso into two, creating the upper thoracic and lower abdominal cavities. We usually think of the diaphragm mostly in connection with its critical function in breathing. The diaphragm's involuntary cycle of alternating contractions and relaxations provides the driving force for the intake of fresh air, and the expelling of used air.

But the diaphragm also plays a very important role in many basic biological processes located in the abdominal cavity. Here, its reflexive contraction can cause a dramatic rise in hydraulic pressure in the abdominal cavity that powers a variety of involuntary eliminative reflexes associated with fundamental bodily functions. Examples are coughing, sneezing, vomiting, urinating, defecating, sexual orgasm, and childbirth. All of them share a general aim and specific method. They all aim to expel or discharge something from the body. And they all utilize the diaphragmatic reflex mechanism to marshal the integrated strength of the lower and upper body to power the eliminative function. For that reason, I will refer to the diaphragm's reflexive contraction in these functions as the "whole body reflex."

This whole body reflex in turn affects the breathing process. When the reflex occurs, it not only compresses the abdominal contents downward, but simultaneously expels the remaining air in the lungs upward and out. This is very evident in how all mammals, including the human species, instinctively use diaphragmatic contraction and the whole body reflex to prepare for action in life-and-death or other crisis situations. In preparation for both fight or flight, forced expiration through the vocal apparatus is released as sound – as in hissing and growling. In flight, the inter-abdominal pressure energy generated by the whole body reflex is discharged through the legs in running; in fighting, the energy is discharged mainly through the upper body in combat thrusts of head, jaw and arms.

Breathing is normally an involuntary reflex activity. "Making the involuntary voluntary" in this context refers to the internal martial arts training in which we learn how to regulate the normal breathing process and adapt it to gain control over the diaphragmatic contraction reflex. Why? Because such control constitutes the very essence of the skill of fajin, the spherical explosive force that we will examine in Part 2.

Stretch and Tendon Reflexes

There are several crisis reflexes that exhibit a yin-yang polarity structure. Developing the specific offensive and defensive skills of the internal martial arts requires cultivating awareness and control over these reflexes. Two of the most primitive of these reflexes are the stretch and tendon reflexes. These two reflexes have opposite, but complimentary, functions in the ongoing process of subconscious, real-time fine-tuning of the web of muscle and connective tissue discussed in the introduction to Book 1.

To understand how these reflexes work, visualize the following two situations. They both entail placing a ball on the palm of a hand held out in front of the waist and then

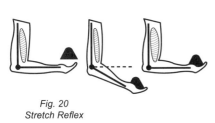

Fig. 20
Stretch Reflex

observing the reaction. In the first situation, unless the ball is too heavy, the ball initially causes the hand to lower and the bounce back up to the original position still holding the added weight (Fig. 20). This is the stretch reflex at work. Specialized cells within the muscles, called "muscle spindles," initiate the stretch reflex and cause the involuntary contraction of the biceps muscle as it is being stretched. They also inhibit the opposing extensor, the triceps muscle. The result is maintenance or recovery of arm position with the added weight. Note the heavier the ball, the greater the distance the palm holding the ball will drop and the greater the effort reqired for the biceps to return the hand to the original position.

Which leads to the second situation in which the weight of the ball is far greater than anticipated and, when placed on the palm, exceeds the capacity of the biceps to maintain the flexing of the arm. As a result, the biceps suddenly releases and the ball drops to the ground (Fig. 21). This

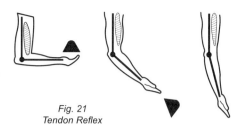

Fig. 21
Tendon Reflex

is the tendon reflex at work. Specialized cells called Golgi organs, present in great numbers in the tendons where they attach to the muscles, initiate the tendon reflex. The tendon reflex causes the involuntary relaxation of the contracting muscle (the agonist). Thus the tendon reflex is the yin to the yang of the stretch reflex.

During standing meditation classes, or as students hold postures from the form, the teacher will often walk around making apparently minor adjustments to the students' stances. The teacher will push a little bit here, pull a little there, exert a little pressure not only on the arms, but also on the sides, the back, or anywhere on the body. During this brief encounter, the teacher gains a lot of information about the students' progress, or lack thereof, in achieving central equilibrium and stability as a result of the standing meditation practice.

Moreover, the teacher is also testing the student's stretch and tendon reflexes. For example, the teacher gives instructions to maintain the structure and not move, and then, while the student is holding the sphere, the teacher applies a small force to the student's arms. At first the student's forearms will be pushed in a little bit toward the chest, and then, when the force is released, they will spring back to the original position. This is the stretch reflex at work. However, when the force applied is greater than the the arms can hold, the spherical structure of the arms will collapse. This is the tendon reflex at work.

As the examples above show, the tendon reflex can override the stretch reflex. Therefore, to prevent the collapse of the sphere's elastic structure, the internal martial artist must become so aware and responsive that an excessive load can never be placed on the body's structure. Only long and careful awareness training achieves this skill.

When the student improves and is able to maintain his frame, neither collapsing nor generating resistance as the teacher pushes on him, it means he is acquiring more voluntary control over the stretch reflex. The stretch and tendon reflexes are involuntary mechanisms that regulate the tension of the tensegrity web. In this context, making the involuntary voluntary means being able to prevent both the stretch and tendon reflex from occurring, and being able to voluntarily regulate the internal tension of the tensegrity web. The next chapter will describe the methodology of doing this. It will also describe how this voluntary control of the internal pressure of our elastic sphere is a key ingredient in the development of both the offensive skill of fajin, the spherical explosive force, as well as the defensive skill of the absorption of energy through postural yielding.

The Opposition/Resistance and Withdrawal/Accommodation Reflexes

Fundamentally, the terms used here - opposition/resistance and withdrawal/ accommodation - describe the two opposite tendencies by which an organism can react to some force trying to dislodge it from its position. These descriptive terms are somewhat arbitrary and I may use one term in the pair or both, as seems to best fit context. In yin-yang terms, the opposition/resistance reflex represents the yang pole of the polarity and the withdrawal/ accommodation reflex represents the yin pole.

Fig. 22
Opposition Reflex

The human species shares the opposition reflex with many animals. Consider what happens when one pushes or leans against a horse, a cow or a dog: the animal invariably resists, pushing back by leaning into the force exerted against it. The reason is simple. The animal is stable; the force attempts to move the animal's center of gravity and destabilize it. Because the animal instinctively wants to remain stable, it pushes back to neutralize the force.[21] Humans are no different. We tend to marshal our physical strength and resist forces acting to displace us from our normal position (Fig. 22). We naturally lean into or push back against a force applied against us.

---

[21] This also explains, by the way, why a harness naturally triggers a mule, ox, horse or dog to pull a cart or sled. The pulling of the harness exerts a force against the animal which it opposes, or resists, by moving forward and thus, moving the load. But if you're in front of the animal and simply try to pull it forward with a rope around its neck, you will witness the opposition reflex; the animal will simply dig in its heels and refuse to go forward.

As the term indicates, the withdrawal/accomodation reflex works in the exact opposite way. Sometimes when pressure is exerted on an organism, it does not resist, but "accomodates" the pressure by moving itself or removing itself and "withdrawing." Pain, or the threat of it, often elicits this reflex- as when one accidentally touches a hot stove.

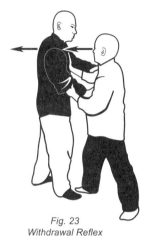

Fig. 23
Withdrawal Reflex

The accomodation/withdrawal reflex also often occurs when the organism perceives on some level that to engage the opposition/ resistance reflex would be futile, or worse, disastrous. Then the organism goes the other way and accommodates itself to the new reality of things by withdrawing (Fig. 23). The accommodation/ withdrawal reflex is characterized by a collapse in physical structure and mental coherence. Its most extreme example is the possum or "playing dead" reflex, which consists of motor inhibition and paralysis in the face of perceived superior force or great danger.

The relevance of this to the internal martial arts, and especially its partner practices called "pushing hands," is profound. Making the involuntary voluntary in this respect entails the transformation of the opposition/resistance reflex into the offensive skills of fajin, and the transformation of the acccommodation/withdrawal reflex into defensive skills of responsiveness and yielding. Making the involuntary voluntary means gaining conscious control over the modulation of the tensegrity structure of our body so that we can bounce and repel an assailant at the merest touch.

There is more. The primary strategy of the internal martial arts is to wait for the opponent to make the first move, then to yield to his attack, and in the process capture his center and cause him to lose balance and to tense, which provides the opportune moment to deliver the fajin. From the perspective of this strategy, learning the skill of yielding requires first unlearning the opposition reflex. Therefore the fundamental purpose of pushing hands training is to replace the opposition/ resistance reflex with the yielding response as the habitual way of dealing with any attempt to apply force on our body.

In addition, while defensively we must completely unlearn and de-activate the opposition reflex in ourselves, offensively, we must learn to induce it in our opponent. By inducing the opposition reflex and then yielding to it, the internal martial artist is able to draw his opponent off balance and capture his central equilibrium.

The chapters that follow will detail how in the game of tuishou (推手) or pushing hands, as in life, the opposition reflex will generally occur before the collapsing reflex. The first impulse will almost always be to resist and push back, and only when the force becomes too great will the accommodation reflex take over and collapse occur. For the internal martial artist, being able to induce either in the opponent will suffice. If one can induce the opposition reflex, the opponent's hard, tense frame gives one access to his central equilibrium; provoke the collapse reflex, and you get direct access to the unprotected body.

The point at which the opposition reflex is supplanted by the collapse reflex is different for every individual and is a function of the relative tone of the muscular and fascial tensegrity web. The more hypertonic, i.e., chronically contracted, the tensegrity web is, the stronger and longer the opposition reflex. Conversely, the more hypotonic, i.e., chronically incapable of strong contraction, the quicker the onset of the collapse reflex. In this respect there seems to be a correlation with gender: men tend more toward opposition reflex while women tend more toward the collapsing reflex.

Flight-Fight Reflexes

The third pair of yin-yang crisis reflexes is the most extreme and intense in terms of function and energy expenditure. These are the flight (yin) and fight (yang) reflexes. Actually, each of these is itself a cascade of neural and hormonal autonomic responses that prepares the body to deal with the highest threat level – one that risks the continued survival of the organism. Moreover, purely reflexive flight-fight instincts are heavily overlaid and supplemented by learned behaviors, or the earlier-mentioned fixed action patterns, allowing for great variations in their expression in individuals.

In the context of these yin-yang crisis reflexes, "making the involuntary voluntary" means nothing less for the internal martial artist than seeking to eliminate this entire range of involuntary crisis behaviors. Cultivation of awareness transforms these polarities into the offensive and defensive skills that define the internal martial arts. Offensively, awareness transforms the yang reflexes (stretch, opposition, fight) into the skills of power and fajin. Defensively, awareness transforms the yin reflexes (tendon, collapse/withdrawal, flight) into the skills of sensitivity and responsiveness, following and yielding.

But eliminating and transforming these involuntary behaviors in oneself is only half of the internal martial artist's objective. The other half consists of acquiring the skills to induce these involuntary yin-yang reflexes in one's opponent. Being able to induce a reflex creates a loss of control in the opponent that gives us a window of opportunity to control the opponent's equilibrium. Inducing the yin reflexes – the tendon reflex, the collapse/withdrawal reflex – will give direct access to the body, while inducing the yang reflexes – the stretch, opposition, or fight reflexes – will induce a tension-filled frame that provides a strong, though indirect, connection to the body's center.

In the final analysis, the best example of making the involuntary voluntary is the body frame. When we lose balance or become startled, or resist, or fight, we reflexively unify the body into a frame for action that is involuntary, rigid and maintained through tension. Standing meditation also integrates the entire body into a whole by unifying sinew, muscle and bone into a structural frame for action, but this frame is voluntary, elastic and maintained through aware relaxation. There are many ways to cultivate this integrity of the frame, but unlike the western approach which focuses on building muscle, the internal martial artist in the eastern tradition focuses, paradoxically, on cultivating awareness of the center.

Part 2

On Jin

Transforming Health into Power

Chapter 4: The Power of the Center

Evolution of the Whole-Body Reflex

In the amoeba (Fig. 24a), the cytoplasmic streamings from the center to the periphery and vice versa are central in regulating the organism's processes of locomotion, digestion, reproduction, and sensation. In amoebic pulsation, expansion and contraction are due to the streamings in the cytoplasm of the thin fluids from the center to the thicker fluids at the periphery, and back from the periphery to the center. These fluid changes are responsible for the elongation and "balling up" phases in locomotion and environment testing. When the pseudopodia (literally, "false feet") extending from an amoeba find a good spot, the entire amoeba moves there; when the spot is found wanting, the amoeba retracts the pseudopodia and moves elsewhere.

Another, slightly more evolved and complex form of this biological pulsation can be observed in swimming jellyfish (Fig. 24b). When a jellyfish moves, it moves from its center, which is the central nerve plexus located in the middle of the back. Undulating from this center, the ends of the body approach and move away from one another in rhythmic interchange. More specifically, in contraction, the ends of the trunk move towards one another in a rhythmic motion, as if they wanted to touch each other, while in relaxation or expansion, they move away from each other.

At each step of the evolutionary ladder, we see this phenomenon of pulsation preserved as the fundamental biological invariant. The starfish (Fig. 24c) and other creatures possessing radial symmetry exhibit yet another type

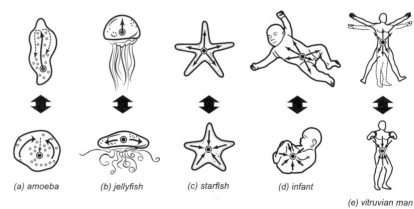

(a) amoeba   (b) jellyfish   (c) starfish   (d) infant

(e) vitruvian man

Fig. 24
The Center as Evolutionary Invariant

of primitive pulsatory movement. Again, the chief characteristic is that all movement of the limbs originates in the center, and then proceeds equally in all directions. The limbs alternate between flexion and extension. At one moment, the limbs draw towards the center, and in the next, they extend out from the center, reaching out and opening into space. The limbs move together and apart, touch and separate. In this way the limbs discover boundaries and the absence of boundaries, and they embody the interaction of the individual parts within the context of unity of the whole.

In evolutionary terms, the bilateral symmetry of all creatures that possess a spine, including the human species, evolved from the radial symmetry of very early life forms, such as the starfish. Indeed, the primitive radially symmetric movement pattern of the starfish is still the dominant pattern of movement *in utero*, and is also still clearly observable in newborn infants, whose movement still emanates from the navel center (Fig. 24d). As an infant throws back its head and/or thrusts out its limbs, either one at the time or in concert with each other, it learns to differentiate and integrate them from a single center.[22] A more adult and artistic representation of the navel radiation pattern in man can be appreciated in Leonardo da Vinci's "The Vitruvian Man," his magnificent drawing and study of the proportions of the human body (Fig. 24e).

...

Even though far evolved beyond the single cell, human life still manifests and conforms to this same primitive fundamental center-to-periphery structure. Like the cell, we have a single center that regulates our growth and other vegetative functions. It is the center of gravity in the human body, as well as the center of integration of our physical strength; and waves of energy propagated in that center radiate out to the periphery. In the cell, such movements involve the hydraulics of the cytoplasm; and in human beings, such movement is mediated by the tensegrity partnership between bones, connective tissue, and muscles. Like the cell, furthermore, we have an outer membrane to our sphere, the skin and senses, through which we interact with the environment.

Like the jellyfish, our pulsatory mechanism also still involves the rhythmic oscillation of the ends of the organism toward each other and away again. It is,

---

[22] Hartley, Linda, "*Wisdom of the Body Moving: An Introduction to Body-Mind Centering,*" North Atlantic Books, Berkeley, CA, 1989, p.29.

in a very literal sense, a "whole-body" reflex that originates in the physical center of the body. In humans, as in all mammals, this is expressed in the way the upper and lower parts of the torso are integrated in expelling or excreting something from the body in the most basic of biological functions like procreation, digestion and locomotion, including flight and fight.

To sum up, the whole of evolution, from the simplest single cell to the most complex organisms, including mammals and human beings, has been characterized by the invariance of a central mechanism for the generation and control of movement. This mechanism is still clearly evident in human movement in utero and infants. In the oriental cultures, moreover, spritual and martial traditions have retained a strong historical connection to and awareness of this biological center. But, sadly, adult human beings in the west have lost their connection with the integrative power of the center. It is one of the purposes of this volume to reawaken us to this connection and gain voluntary control over it.

The Center in Eastern Traditions

In March 2007, the *San Jose Mercury News* reported that Stanford researchers had recorded the striking power of a famous Beijin taiji master.[23] Working on the classical formulation that "force equals mass times acceleration," the Stanford scientists hooked the master up to their instruments and found his strikes were able to generate 400 pounds of force by an acceleration from 0-60 mph in 2.8 seconds. As the newspaper pointed out, the explosive force of the master's fajin exceeded the acceleration of any Lamborghini on the street.

This is the art of fajin, the spherically explosive pulse of power, considered by many to be the pinnacle of martial achievement. In the sections that follow, we'll assume that after training as described in Part 1, we all have acquired the proper habits of posture, breathing and movement needed to cultivate the qi. That is to say, we've all improved our systemic health and integration to the point that we can proceed with learning how to focus that health and energy to acquire the skill of fajin. The pulse begins in the abdominal center and is propagated spherically, that is, in all directions, throughout the body's elastic frame. But no matter how devastating fajin can be, there are limits to its awesome power. Thus, when we understand these limits

---

[23] San Jose Mercury News, 05/03/2007.

and accept them, we can begin to develop other skills that are still more powerful and subtle, enabling us to respond effectively to a a variety of difficult challenges.

...

In the East, many traditions throughout the millennia have described and cultivated the abdomen as the physical center of human well-being and power. Yogis, Buddhists and especially the asian martial arts traditions seek to train and develop the power of the center, called hara in Japanese, or dantian in Chinese. In the West, however, while we might seek a strong core or washboard abs, there's no culture or tradition of cultivating the power of the center. Dr. David Eisenberg's account was illustrative of the lack of western knowledge on the subject. After meeting with Chinese medical doctors and qigong practitioners in the early days of China's opening up to the West, Eisenberg reported in astonishment:

> People practicing qi gong say ... they can feel the energy Qi in the pit of their stomach, in the dantian point below their navel. They can move it. It's real to them. It is not a concept, but something they can feel, push, pull ... Qi is a physical entity and not merely a conceptual construct ... a biophysical reality which remains undefined, having eluded present day biotechnology.[24]

What so baffled Eisenberg — the physical reality of accumulated qi in the abdomen — is nothing more (or less) than the process of the unconscious becoming conscious. In qigong, mindful breathing practices, both natural and reverse, bring awareness and voluntary control over the previously involuntary abdominal musculature. Being able to move the abdominal muscles at will in circular and spherical movement patterns, the practitioner creates a (mostly tactile) sensation that quite feels like the rolling of a ball. The true master can vary the inter-abdominal pressure as needed along an entire spectrum of exertion, so that the abdomen can change, instantly going from pliant and non-resistant to an iron-hardness, and vice versa.

I have observed this spectrum repeatedly in Master Tam's demonstrations. I recall the experience of one student, a professional boxer, as he tried to push Master Tam's abdomen. Master Tam kept yielding, controlling the student's hand with his

---

[24] David Eisenberg, M.D. and Ted Kapchuk,"What is Qi," C.A.A. Newsletter, June 1987. See also, David Eisenberg, M.D., "Encounters With Qi: Exploring Chinese Medicine," Penguin Books, New York, NY,1985.

abdominal muscles by varying the pressure in his belly. The student was unable to effectively push or strike, until finally, he gave up, exclaiming: "What the hell do you have in there, an animal?"

At the other end of the spectrum, I have felt Master Tam's abdomen when he is using inter-abdominal pressure for sinking the qi and fajin discharge, and it can be hard as a rock. I have also witnessed martial artists from a variety of disciplines trying their utmost to punch Master Tam in the abdomen to no avail. Either they are bounced back to where they came from or they crumple to the ground grabbing a painful wrist.

That's no exaggeration. Depending on the skill and intent of the issuer, the attacker may experience any number of neutralizing and quite unexpected responses. Someone who throws a punch may experience a short and sharp penetrating force upon making contact. She may feel that her force is being absorbed and then bounced back, as if by a trampoline or shot from a slingshot. Whatever the case, at the moment of the act, at the center of the issuance of the force, one can feel the abdomen of the master become hard and firm. The "iron bell"—that is the term in Chinese internal arts classics for the belly that is hard and strong as metal. I call it the "dome of power."

Dantian: The Dome of Power

Since time immemorial, the holy grail of the Chinese martial artist has been to develop fajin, the explosive internal power that throughout history has been

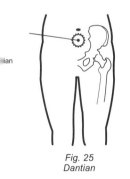

Fig. 25
Dantian

pursued by many while realized by few. The masters who wrote the classics describe this force as generated in the abdominal area called the dantian, meaning "cinnabar field" that is the area of concentrated qi power just below the navel. Professor Zheng Manqing described its location as 2-3 finger widths below the navel and two finger widths inside (Fig. 25). Professor Zheng emphasized that as the power area, the dantian is indistinguishable from the body's center of gravity, which is also the same as "what Taijiquan calls 'central equilibrium.'"[25]

[25] Douglas, Wile, ed., *"Chen Man-Ch'ing's Advanced T'ai-Chi Form Instructions: With Selected Writings on Meditation, The I Ching, Medicine and the Arts,"* Sweet Ch'i Press, New York, 1985, p. 50.

Li Ts'un-i , a famous Xing-I master, expressed it in these words: "When you stand still, keep everything to the navel; when you move, energy shoots out from the navel with obvious and concealed energy."[26]

My own hands-on experience with Master Tam, and to a lesser extent my own internal development, corroborate these descriptions by the old masters. After long cultivation, a tremendous energy (qi) accumulates in the dantian area. When relaxed, this abdominal area feels like an elastic ball if palpated, but at the moment of the issuance of fajin, it becomes rounded like a dome and hard as a rock. And, like everyone else who I've talked to who has felt this "dome of power," my own reaction upon first feeling it was something like: "Holy cow!" I wondered about the nature of this hardness and how is it produced.

Clearly, it is not caused by a contraction of the rectus abdominis and the transverse abdominal musculature—that would pull the abdominal contents in and flatten the abdomen. The "dome of power" feels like the abdominal contents are trying to push through and burst out of the abdominal wall. And in fact this is the case. The perception of the dantian area as an expanding dome of power is caused by the stretch reflex of the abdominal muscles.

Recall that the stretch reflex is perhaps one of the most basic and primitive reflexes of them all. It operates entirely on a subconscious level as a spinal chord reflex. It acts as a safety mechanism that prevents a muscle from being stretched and torn by the opposite member of its pair. In this case it is the contracting diaphragm that elicits the stretch reflex in the abdominal muscles as they resist being stretched suddenly and powerfully.[27]

Biomechanically, what happens is that the mind (with or without use of the breath) tells the diaphragm to contract. This causes the diaphragm to push down and increase the hydraulic pressure in the abdominal cavity.

---

[26] Robert W. Smith, "*Hsing-I, Chinese Mind-Body Boxing*," Kodansha International, Tokyo, New York & San Francisco, 1974, p.103.

[27] I am indebted to Dr. Samuel Dismond III of San Francisco for first pointing this out to me. Private communication, 10/27/2006.

Constrained on the back side by the spine and on the down side by the pelvic floor, the increase in hydraulic pressure consequently causes expansion of the abdominal wall mostly forward and, to a lesser extent, sideways. This activates the stretch reflex in the abdominal musculature to create the dome of power.

Anatomically, the dantian area corresponds to the arcuate line (Fig. 26), the horizontal line of demarcation that runs across the abdomen, below the navel and above the pubic bone. Above it, the rectus abdominis passes in front of the fascial sheet made up of the flat, broad tendons of all three abdominal muscles: the external obliques, the internal obliques, and the transversus abdominis. Below it, on its way to attachment to the pubic bone,

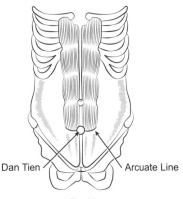

Dan Tien   Arcuate Line

Fig. 26
Dantien and Arcuate Line

the rectus abdominis passes behind, and is covered by, the same fascial sheet. This arrangement provides for maximum structural strength and integrity. Interwoven, intersecting muscle layers are stronger than the same two sheets merely covering each other, and are strongest at the point of intersection, which is the most likely reason it is experienced as the locus or center of physical power.

The skill of fajin, the spherically explosive force, is a special case of transforming the involuntary "whole body reflex" into something voluntary—and immensely powerful. The subconscious partnership of locomotive and respiratory crisis functions is made the conscious cornerstone of the internal martial artist's skill and strategy; through volitional action, the upper and lower trunks are integrated with each other and with their extremities. It is precisely through standing and moving meditation that the "whole body reflex" of animal crisis behavior is transformed into the zhengti (整體), the "coherent body" of the internal martial arts.

The Practice of Reverse Breathing

In Chapter 2 we saw that the first step of the aspiring internal martial artist's journey is about transformation of normal into natural breathing, and with it, ill health into good health.

When this has been achieved, the next step of training and experience involves a second transformation, this time of the natural breathing pattern into what is called the "reverse breathing" pattern. Reverse breathing provides the method for transforming the internal martial artist's newfound health into martial power. Reverse breathing practice leads to the ability to issue jin, or explosive power. It entails training the center to learn direct, voluntary control over the diaphragmatic function of the whole-body reflex in order to generate, at will, the pulse of fajin power.

Natural and reverse breathing are inherently related and complement each other. Natural breathing is for energy cultivation, and reverse breathing is for energy use. Thus natural breathing is the root and foundation of reverse breathing. Let's examine this more closely.

In natural breathing, at the end of the exhalation, there is a volume of air that remains in the lungs and is not expelled before the next inhale commences. Technically referred to as ERV (Expiratory Reserve Volume), this extra air becomes important when a load is placed on the system, and the breath is called upon to help power and integrate the motor effort necessary to overcome the resistance. At such a moment the diaphragm contracts powerfully. This has the effect of (1) pulling the pelvic floor and tail bone under, to integrate the strength of spine and legs into effort and (2) expelling the ERV forcefully, often by means of powerful vocalizations.

The effect of the powerful diaphragmatic contraction on the muscles of the abdominal wall is fascinating. As the contents of the abdominal cavity are forcefully pushed down the resulting increase in pressure causes the sudden stretching of the abdominal muscles outward. This stretching in turn activates the stretch reflex in the abdominal muscles causing them to contract and tighten to prevent their further stretching. The net result of increased pressure in a decreased volume makes the abdomen round as a balloon and firm as a basketball.

The load placed on the system to cause such an effect need not be large. Sneezing and coughing are two involuntary reflexes that can provide direct experiential verification of this claim and description. The next time you sneeze or cough, just put your hand on your tummy and you will feel the sudden contraction of the diaphragm cause a pulse of energy that, going up, expels what the sneeze and cough want to expel, and going down, expands the abdominal wall, which tightens involuntarily to contain it.

Reverse Breathing

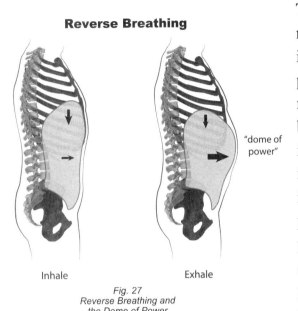

"dome of power"

Inhale   Exhale

Fig. 27
Reverse Breathing and
the Dome of Power

The ancient Chinese sages observed such naturally occurring events with keen interest and adapted the basic principles involved in the "reverse breathing" methodology for power training. Reverse breathing is a kind of forced expiration in which the abdominal wall is pulled in, or deflated, during the inhalation and is actively pushed out, or inflated, to expand in the exhalation. They called the practice "reverse breathing" because during the inhalation the abdomen is pulled in (as opposed to pushing out in natural breathing) and during the exhalation it is pushed out to power movement and effort (as opposed to pulling in on the exhale in natural breathing) (Fig. 27).

*The **stillness** of standing meditation is particularly conducive to beginning the practice of reverse breathing. On the exhalation, one expands the sphere equally from the abdominal center to the six directions: down and up, forward and backward, and sideways left and right. The forward expansion of the dantian in the belly is balanced with the backward expansion of the mingmen (命門) in the back. Half the energy can be felt sinking down into the feet for grounding stability and movement agility, while the other half extends out to the arms or other point of contact for yielding and possible discharge. On the inhalation, the procedure is reversed and the energy is drawn from the six directions into the dantian.*

*In the next higher level of reverse breathing, the torso **moves** in each spatial dimension separately: while moving up-down in the vertical dimension, shifting front-back* *in the horizontal dimension and rotating clockwise-counterclockwise in the left-right dimension. Finally, in the highest level of accomplishment, one uses the exhalation in reverse breathing to power the simultaneous oppositional expansion of all three spatial polarities to generate the spherical expansion of the fajin pulse from the dantian. Possible movements of trunk and arms in spherical and circular orbits are numerous. Ranging from big to small, and from slow to fast, with the internal resistance itself varying from maximum to minimum, there are an infinite number of possible combinations.*

For reverse breathing to work and produce fajin, two requirements must be met. The first is that the abdominal muscles be completely relaxed. The second requirement is that the spine be kept meticulously straight and remain lengthened (as in "natural" exhalation) during both inhale and exhale. As Yang Chengfu put it, only "when the abodomen relaxes completely...then the energy collects in the bones,"[28] particularly the spine. So, no washboard tummies allowed here. Indeed, the more relaxed the abdominal musculature, the more the stretch receptors are able to fire and increase the strength of the contraction, thereby producing an increasingly prominent "dome of power" effect.[29]

Generally speaking, for health maintenance and the cultivation of spherical force, movements are larger and slower. In fajin, however, movements are smaller and faster. In this respect, Wang Xiangzhai's words bear repeating again: "Small movement is better than big movement; no movement is better than small movement."

The *ability* to generate power in the abdominal center does not assure that power *will be* delivered. If one cannot maintain the proper body frame, the power pulse will not be expressed or effectively directed at the target. The frame is crucial: it must be elastic, and that is an art unto itself.

---

[28] Yang Chengfu, the Brennan translation, op.cit.

[29] A word of caution here: because reverse breathing and internal oppositional exertion practices can be quite physically taxing, it is wise not to engage in this type of training when one is tired or sick, but only when one is feeling well.

Chapter 5: The Frame Elastic

Internal Martial Arts and Elastic Strength

Since the beginning of history, the western way of thinking about health and physical fitness has always put the development of muscular strength at a premium. In sharp contrast, the Chinese way of thinking and training has tended to regard muscular development as merely the first and elemental stage of strength development—the stage of overt and obvious strength. Development in the internal martial arts is characterized by the transformation of this hard, overt strength in the muscles and bones into its opposite: a soft, subtle, elastic force, associated with the connective tissues of tendons, ligaments and fascia.

Historical documentation of this eastern view dates back at least to the Bodidharma, who lived circa 500 C.E. and created the Muscle/Tendon Changing Classic (Yi Jin Jing, 易筋經) and Bone Marrow Cleansing Classic (Xi Sui Jing, 洗髓經). Yi Jin Jing is a series of 12 exercises, performed in a standing position, that utilize simultaneous exertion of opposing muscle groups. Allowing no jerky movements or overstraining, the exercises are performed sometimes with effort and vigor, sometimes smoothly and gently, but always harmonizing movement with the breath. There are many other similar forms of exercise such as the Five Animal Frolics, the Iron Shirt, the Eight Brocades (Ba Duan Gin, 八段錦), etc.

These exercises, as well as many martial disciplines, seek to cultivate the qi to improve the health and well-being of the tendons, ligaments and other parts of the fascial web. Specifically, the traditional eastern view is that practicing these exercises mobilizes and stores qi in and between the various layers of the fascia throughout the body. This storage of qi between the fascial layers acts at the same time as a protective cushion of resilient tissue and energy.

Twentieth-century masters such as Professor Zheng Manqing and Master Wang Xiangzhai continued to express this point of view. Quoting Li Yiyu approvingly,

Professor Zheng refers to the contractile muscle strength as force while referring to elastic connective tissue strength as energy (qi): "Energy and force are not the same. Energy comes from the sinews and force from the bones… Qi originates in the sinews, blood vessels, membranes, and diaphragm."[30] The Yang family manuscripts likewise read: "Qi runs in the channels of the internal membranes and sinews. Those who possess qi have internal strength in their sinews … Qi and blood work to strengthen the internal. Mobilizing qi in the sinews and using strength in the skin and bones are two vastly different things."[31]

Grandmaster Wang Xiangzhai describes how proper training creates a kind of positive feedback loop between the bones (as the rigid compression members) and the connective tissue (as the tensile members) of our body's tensegrity structure. "When the ligaments are stretched and elongated," he wrote, "the bones become heavy and dense" and then "their strength is increased."[32] And the effect is reciprocal: "When the bones become dense and heavy, the ligaments become agile."[33] As this process deepens and the connective tissues becomes stronger and more elastic, the bones themselves become more flexible, and their strength, and the total tensile strength of the body's tensegrity structure, increases accordingly. "When the bones become flexible," he wrote, "then their strength has substance and solidity … and is transported through the ligaments."[34]

The Center and the Frame

Karlfried Graf Durkheim summarized the eastern conception of the relationship of the center to the body's overall structure as follows: "The tanden [dantian], the area below the navel, is the center of man. The art of activating it is to release the strength of all the other parts of the body and concentrate it there."[35] These "other parts of the body" are none other than the six arms of the prenatal navel radiation movement pattern discussed previously (Fig. 24): the head and tail, the two arms and the two legs.

---

[30] "*Zheng Manqing Cheng's 13 Chapters,*" op. cit., p. 64.

[31] Douglas Wile, "*T'ai-chi Touchstones: Yang Family Secret Transmissions,*" Sweet Ch'I Press, New York, p.86.

[32] Wang Xiangzhai, "*The Right Path of Yiquan,*" op.cit., p. 8.

[33] Ibid.

[34] Ibid.

[35] Karlfried Graf Durckheim, "*Hara: The Vital Center of Man,*" Inner Traditions, Rochester, Vermont,1956, p. 192.

This connection between the center and the extremities is clearly indicated by the near-identical language used by a modern-day physical therapist describing the pre-natal navel radiation pattern, and the training instructions of an internal martial arts grandmaster. Linda Hartley, a leading body-mind investigator writes: "At this earliest stage of pre- and post-natal development, movement is organized around the navel center; from here it radiates through all six limbs of the head, tail, arms and legs."[36] Compare this with Grandmaster Wang Xiangzhai's instructions:

> In stretching and strengthening tendons and bones spherically, the six centers (two hands, the two feet, the body center and the skull center), must all coordinate with each other… to stretch the ligaments, stretch the neck, the two wrists and the two ankles. When this is done all the ligaments in the body will be elongated… (and) stretch your bones like the strings of a bow, enabling you to recoil and use your intrinsic strength (jin) fully.[37]

Now recall how in the discussion of primitive reflexes we saw that the involuntary, innate reactions of the body to threat are either to tighten through tension into a rigid frame, or to collapse altogether. In between these extremes of involuntary reaction lies the happy medium of voluntary response. Between rigid and collapsed frames, there is the middle way of the elastic frame. The internal martial arts train to make the elastic frame a voluntary response, and to control that elasticity for offensive and defensive uses. Seen in this light, the six-direction training of the internal martial arts bestows on the practitioner nothing less than the conscious mastery of the innate naval radiation pattern. It integrates the four limbs, the head, and the tail, through the dantian power center into the voluntary elastic frame.

Voluntary command over the frame gives the internal martial artist the ability to exploit the inherent vulnerabilities of the rigid or collapsed frames that result from involuntary crisis reflexes. In an opponent, both excessive tension and excessive looseness throughout the frame or at any one particular point (i.e., a joint) constitute vulnerabilities that can be attacked.

---

[36] Linda Hartley, *"Wisdom of the Body Moving: An Introduction to Body-Mind Centering,"* North Atlantic Books, Berkeley, CA, 1989, p. 30.

[37] Wang Xiangzhai, op.cit., p. 8.

For example, the lumbar region where the upper and lower torsos connect is highly vulnerable. And so is the cervical region, where the head is integrated with the torso. The same holds true for the shoulder girdle, where the arms connect with the torso, as well as at the shoulders, elbows, and wrists that integrate the sphere of the arms. Further vulnerability exists in the hips, where the legs (foundation) integrate with the torso, and in the hips, knees and ankles that constitute the sphere of the foundation.

In what way, precisely, are rigid and collapsed frames vulnerable? A collapsed structure is like a leak in a ball; in defense, it gives no protection and allows direct access to the centerline and the body, while on offense, a collapsed structure cannot propagate the fajin pulse. The involuntary rigid frame—whether in an isolated joint or in the whole body—is also disastrous for internal martial arts uses. Defensively, the rigidity gives your opponent access to your central equilibrium and the opportunity to deliver the fajin to the center, while offensively, an involuntary rigid frame cannot generate a voluntary fajin pulse.

Over time, the internal martial arts six-direction training creates a particular body frame in the practitioner. The defining characteristic of this body frame is the voluntary modulation of its elastic nature. In the case of an accomplished artist such as Master Tam, the tensegrity structure is nearly flawless. Offensively, because there are no breaks in his frame, the energy pulse originating at his center propagates through his body instantaneously, and without wind-up is discharged at the point of contact into the opponent. Defensively, any force directed to his body is absorbed and redirected, thereby preventing any access to his centerline.

The Frame as Energy Storage System

As we have seen, the partnership of bone, connective tissue and muscle maintains our posture and enables our movement. As the organ of form, the connective tissue web literally connects the muscles to the bones and holds both in place; when stretched, the web stores energy until it is released. Muscles, being contractile in nature, are the active adjusting mechanism that regulates the elasticity of the connective tissue by stretching and relaxing it in posture and movement. Thus muscle, when contracting, besides pulling the bones as fulcrums and levers to produce movement, also stretches the tendons, fascia and other components of the connective tissue web. But due to the elastic nature of the connective tissue web, whenever it is stretched, connective tissue stores energy and uses it to partially power subsequent actions.

To understand better how this energy-storing mechanism works, let's revisit the kangaroo's bipedal hopping method of locomotion. The kangaroo has developed tremendously powerful elastic tendons in its legs. These tendons are so efficient in absorbing and storing energy that up to 80 percent of the energy generated by gravity each time a kangaroo lands is used to power the next jump. This means that as kangaroos jump faster and higher and further, their energy consumption actually increases in efficiency. Relatively speaking, at higher speeds, they need to use less muscle energy to cover long distances.

The internal martial artist seeks to strengthen the tendon structure of her entire body to increase her capacity for receiving, absorbing, rebounding and reissuing her opponent's energy with less and less effort. At least three conditions must be satisfied before someone can control opponents with such ease and finesse as Master Tam does: the central equilibrium, the elastic frame and the awareness must all be highly developed. If the kangaroo lands off balance, its energy is dissipated and cannot be used to power the next hop. Likewise, the central equilibrium and vertical stability of the internal martial artist must be absolutely intact and uncompromised before the body can act as a stable trampoline that absorbs an opponent's energy and bounces it back.

The connective tissue's elastic strength, by the way, also explains the lack of fatigue on the part of those who have mastered it. Master Tam, for instance, can bounce people all day and not get tired. His breathing always remains even and he is never out of breath, even as each challenger one after the other, huffing and puffing, gives way for the next one. Why? With muscular strength, by contracting the muscles, one uses one's own strength. When one is using tendon strength, one uses the force and energy of one's opponent to stretch the tendons, loading and storing the opponent's energy in one's tendons, stretching them as if they were elastic bands, and then releasing that energy back toward its origin, the opponent.

Developing the Frame

Most everyday activities and exercises, such as pushing, pulling, lifting objects, doing sit-ups, throwing a ball or swinging a bat, involve what is called isotonic muscular contraction, in which the muscle shortens as it contracts. "Iso" means equal, and "tonic" refers to the intensity of the effort, so that isotonic simply means that the strength of the contraction determines (i.e., equals) the amount of shortening in the muscle. Much less common, and the opposite of isotonic contraction, is eccentric muscular contraction. In this type of effort, the muscle actually lengthens as it gains tension. For example, someone manages to pull your arm straight while at the same time you are trying to flex it. In other words, the load is too great. In this case, the biceps is experiencing eccentric contraction. Other examples include the muscular contractions that occur as we're running downhill, walking downstairs or landing on the ground from a jump.

In the very beginning stages of internal martial arts training, as in learning the mechanics of the taiji form, any exertion will be isotonic and minimal because in addition to learning the sequence, one must learn to relax. Normal isotonic movement operates according to what is called the "reciprocal innervation" principle. This simply means that contraction by an agonist muscle automatically initiates the simultaneous relaxation of its corresponding antagonist.

For example, in the human leg, when the quadraceps acts to extend the lower leg, biceps femoris automatically relaxes. Conversely when the biceps femoris acts to flex the lower leg, the quadraceps relaxes (Fig. 28).

Fig. 28
Reciprocal Innervation of Muscle Pairs

At the higher levels of training in stillness and movement, the internal martial arts do away with the principle of reciprocal enervation, in which the contraction of the agonist automatically relaxes the antagonist, and vice versa. Instead, the principle of internal oppositional exertion becomes paramount. In this more advanced practice both agonist and antagonist contract simultaneously – the first isotonically in shortening and the latter eccentrically in lengthening – in effect they work against each other and create a dynamic tension between the paired muscles.

In this state of being and movement, there is no extension without some flexion, and there is no flexion without some extension. There is no effort without a counter-effort contained within it. This is Wang Xiangzhai's concept of zhengti (coherent body), in which the "muscles are as one," with extensors and flexors acting simultaneously as both agonist and antagonist. In standing, their contractions are equal, and they will cancel each other out: there will be no outward visible movement. Inwardly, however, there may be a lot of exertion taking place with each muscle contracting and stretching simultaneously to create the dynamic stillness so apparent in the correct postural practice of the internal martial arts. Since there is no movement of the joints, and no change in the length of any muscle, this type of practice can properly be described as internal oppositional exertion.

This use of oppositional exertion is one of the cornerstones of effective internal martial arts strength and movement training. What is required to incorporate this principle successfully in internal martial arts training is, more than anything, a mental shift in awareness and thinking from uni-directional intentionality to an intentionality that embraces polarity.

In the simplest formulation, in internal martial arts strength training, the effort made to accomplish something only slightly exceeds the effort exerted internally to prevent it from being accomplished. Because such omni-directional, mutually canceling efforts engage the connective tissue web continually, they increase the elastic strength of the frame even while an external observer discerns no apparent movement.

Grandmaster Wang taught that through "six-direction training," all the muscles of the body begin to act together as one muscle to produce the pulse of fajin power. We are now in a better position to understand the why and how of this truth: exertion within the frame means to exert within the context of the six direction polarity structure of the body in space. To maintain central equilibrium, any exertion must be constrained by its opposite. As Yang Luchan, the founder of the Yang style of taiji, wrote, "With an upward comes a downward, with a forward comes a backward, and with a left comes a right."[38] Thus, "If your intention wants to go upward, then harbor a downward intention."[39] Likewise, for any forward exertion, there must be backward exertion, For any leftward exertion, there must be rightward exertion, and so on. Becoming aware of and training the three polarity exertions is sequential at first, and then later becomes simultaneous. That is, the front-back, left-right, and top-bottom polarities are each practiced individually before coming together in the skill of spherical awareness and expansion.

To integrate the center with the frame, often internal oppositional exertion is practiced simultaneously with reverse breathing. *As you exhale, feel the simultaneous inflation of the abdominal dome and six directional expansion of the body sphere. With every breath, consciously train the diaphragm at the center to mimic the Whole Body Reflex, unifying the upper and lower body in generating and propagating the pulse of jin. Feel how the energy splits; some is sent to the legs to stabilize the foundation, while the rest spreads evenly throughout the body for discharge from any point of the body.*

---

[38] Yang Chengfu [and Dong Yingjie], "*Methods of Applying Taiji Boxing*," translated by Paul Brennan, Nov 2011.
   http://brennantranslation.wordpress.com/2011/11/24/methods-of-applying-taiji-boxing-taiji-quan-shiyong-fa/
[39] Ibid.

Moving the Frame

The equal exertion of opposing muscle groups creates dynamic stillness: if I contract my biceps and triceps equally, there will be no movement of the arm. When there is unequal exertion of opposing muscle groups, there is movement: if I contract my biceps more than my triceps, the arm will flex and move. Thus, to the extent that the opposing contractions are unequal, there will be movement in the direction of the stronger contraction, with the lesser contraction of the opposite member acting as a brake on the movement. In this case, the contraction of the agonist, because it is getting shorter, is isotonic, while the contraction of the antagonist, because it is getting longer, is eccentric.

In order to strengthen the elasticity of the connective tissue web through movement, you must engage in movement as if someone is restraining you from making that movement. For example, applied to the horizontal movement of the torso, this means that when shifting forward, the forward force of the rear foot pushing is countered by an almost equal force of the front foot pushing back and resisting. In walking, when placing the foot in a step forward, the foot has to first touch the ground and establish an oppositional relationship between the legs before the center/weight can be shifted forward. As in moving the centerline and torso horizontally, so it is moving vertically and rotationally: the effort exerted to move in one direction is resisted by the effort to move in the opposite direction.

Likewise, consider the movement of the arms as they define the sphere of our extension in space. In the vertical movement of the arms, while lifting the hands, imagine that something is exerting an almost equal force in the opposite direction to prevent their upward movement. Or when lowering the arms/hands from a high position, feel as if you're pushing two balls down into the water; the lower you push, the greater the resistance you feel.

In the horizontal movement of the arms, when extending the arms in front of the body and pushing out, the effort forward is resisted by the biceps pulling back, and is counterbalanced as well by a backward expansion in the shoulders.

When flexing the arms as if pulling something towards you, feel as if you're be-ing held back from doing so. Likewise, when opening the arms sideways to the left and right, feel as if you're pulling elastic bands that connect the fingers, and when closing them, feel as if you're squeezing a ball between the palms.

In the rotational movement of arms, get a feel for the idea this way: extend an arm and ask someone to hold your wrist tight while you turn the forearm. Emphasize they're not to hold you so tight as to immobilize you. Pay attention to the feeling of turning the forearm against the external resistance. Then ask your friend to remove her hand from your wrist. Now turn the forearm again, imagining that your friend is still holding your wrist and that you are turning against her force. Now you have replaced the external resistance with internal resistance and your imagination has activated the antagonist to resist the agonist. The rotational movement of the arms is most often used in conjunction with, and as an extension of, the rotation of the body. The oppositional principle applied here is the same: when rotating the torso and/or arms one way, imagine a force that is wanting to rotate them the opposite way.

Practicing the Frame

The intensity of movement practice, and of stillness for that matter, can be at any point along a spectrum of internal oppositional exertion from very light to very heavy. The criteria for when to practice in a light way and when to practice in a heavy way comes from understanding the objective of each. Heavy is for strength and power training, while light is for sensitivity and response training. Daily practice depends on preference and feeling. As with reverse breathing, it is common sense to engage in oppositional internal strength training only when you're feeling up and well; if you're down, unwell or tired, just move very lightly without exertion.

The developmental progression of "growing" an elastic frame, proceeds from an initial stage of having no frame through a middle stage of having a too-heavy frame to the advanced stage of having an ultra-light frame.

In the middle stage, students will want to put more internal oppositional resistance in their movements to stretch and strengthen the frame's elasticity for the cultivation and delivery of power. Many practitioners get stuck in this stage; as a result their frames become rigid and stiff, their movement slow and heavy. Therefore, in the higher stages, internal martial artists will go in the opposite direction and practice with lighter and lighter internal effort. Ultimately, they maintain their frames and their readiness not with strength, but with awareness only. It is this light, elastic frame that gives the internal martial artist agility and explosiveness.

In the larger context of the pushing-hands game, bouncing and uprooting occur when one player is able to capture the center of gravity and balance of another player. In this case, let's call them Jill and Jack. Let's say Jill, either through yielding or sticking, has succesfully captured Jack's center, causing Jack to loose balance and stiffen involuntarily. Jack's involuntary frame allows Jill to discharge her fajin into Jack and send him flying. The difference between bouncing and uprooting is this. Bouncing is when the opponent is hurled back very fast, walking or stumbling but yet with one foot generally still in contact with the ground. Uprooting is a higher level skill in which both feet of the opponent completely leave the ground.

Internal martial artists use cooperative bouncing and uprooting practices as a laboratory for developing awareness and control over the elasticity of the frame, and the delivery of the fajin or explosive spherical force. The laboratory setting of the practice is such that the bouncing and uprooting drills are initially done on a stationary target, a non-moving person. At a beginning level, the target may present the bouncer with a rigid frame. This simulates the moment in the pushing hands game when one's center is captured, and one experiences loss of balance or awareness, causing an involuntary stiffening reflex. On a more advanced level, the target will not present the bouncer with a rigid frame; rather the bouncer must induce it through awareness and technique.

Fig. 29
Bouncing Practice

This structured bouncing practice gives students an opportunity to learn the sensations of proper pulse generation at the center and fajin delivery at the point of contact. Bouncing and uprooting practice (Fig. 29) lead to voluntary control over the variables of the pulse and the frame—the angle, force and velocity of the energy discharge, and the distance over which it is projected. This practice also cultivates development of the muscles working as one, maintaining appropriate tension in the tendons and fascia as the energy moves through the elastic frame in six directions.

The Limits of Power

The yin (defense) and yang (offense) sides of the internal martial arts curriculum are the expressions of the fundamental charge-discharge formula of biological pulsation. The elastic nature of our tensegrity structure gives us a dual capacity. First, as we have seen in this chapter, the yang aspect gives us the ability to inflate and expand our frame outwardly by a pulse of power generated internally, in the dantian. Secondly, the yin aspect gives us the ability to receive external forces and either divert them or absorb and store them internally. In other words, the defense side of the curriculum consists not of power training, but of responsiveness training.

When it comes to evaluating the relative difficulty of mastering each side, Master Tam always says that the yin, or responsiveness, skills are four times more difficult to master than the power skills of fajin. We can add to this the further observation that mastery of the responsiveness skills enhances by four times at least the efficacy of the power skills. Responsiveness has two elements: awareness (of the thing we are responding to), which is neuro-sensory, or perceptual, in nature, and the response itself, which is neuro-motor, or muscular, in nature.

In an evolutionary sense, the paradigm shift in the martial arts from external to internal seems to have mirrored the very evolution of life itself. In the short term at least, the undeniable biological truth is that, growing bigger, stronger and more powerful bodies bestows greater survival advantage on the individual and species as compared to its smaller and weaker members. Martial arts, accordingly, have by tradition focused their efforts on training for physical strength and power. But from a longer evolutionary perspective, the emergence of human intelligence (awareness) has proved of even greater survival value than strength and power. For internal martial arts theory, likewise, victory or defeat are not a function of size and strength, but a function of responsiveness, i.e., motor response governed by awareness and not by reflex. For this reason, only the internal martial arts hold the hope of victory for the smaller and weaker. If a small person is more aware and responsive, she can defeat a larger and stronger one.

With respect to the skill of delivering the fajin power pulse, one must also ask the following question. From the point of view of the issuer, what is it that directs this deadly force? Or to put the question another way, what assures that the force will hit its intended target? The answer is obvious: without perception and awareness, such power is blind. Only perception and awareness can assure that the force will be delivered at the time and place intended, that the sequence of events is "ready, aim, fire", and not "ready, fire, aim." And from the intended recipient's point of view, one can ask what, if anything, can be done to counter such a force? The answer is the same: only perception and awareness can be developed as an antidote to ensure that such a force never reaches its intended target, the centerline. Thus, in the end, for the internal martial artist, all conflict is a conflict of awareness, and the development of awareness becomes the highest pursuit.

Sadly, it must be said that the development of most internal martial artists stops with the development of the offensive skill of fajin. For a variety of reasons, most fail to evolve beyond the neuro-motor integration to develop the skills of neuro-sensory integration. Failure to compliment the yang with the yin means one's internal martial art will forever remain incomplete and limited to the use of strength. For the fundamental operating premise of the internal martial arts is precisely that the use of strength (force) and awareness are inversely proportional: the less awareness a person has, the more force will be needed to control an opponent. And the corollary: the more awareness a person develops, the less force will be required to control an opponent.

The lack of sensory integration and awareness turns the martial artist's neuro-motor integration from an asset into a liability. Those who develop little or no skill in modulating their power tend to have very little control – their force operates with an on-off switch. The disadvantages of this are obvious. For one, if matched against a similar opponent, such lack of awareness and power modulation easily leads to people getting hurt unintentionally and unnecessarily. Secondly, when matched against martial artists with highly developed integration of sensory awareness and motor responses, those who fail to develop these skills are at a severe disadvantage.

Book 2
The Embodied Mind
Mental Faculties Controlling Somatic Functions

Introduction to Book Two:
Parameters of the Nervous System

Voluntary and Involuntary

The nervous system animates the machinery of bone, muscle and connective tissue that holds the body together in a structure and enables its movement. Motor activity is the result of the neural output of the brain as central processor (Fig. 30); the inputs are the neural data streams from the various senses. Because they connect the periphery of the body with the center, the neural streams of sensory input and motor output are often referred to as the

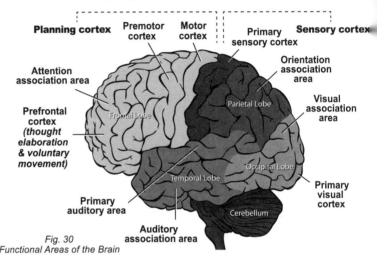

Planning cortex Premotor cortex Motor cortex Primary sensory cortex Sensory cortex

Attention association area

Orientation association area

Prefrontal cortex (thought elaboration & voluntary movement)

Parietal Lobe

Frontal Lobe

Visual association area

Occipital Lobe

Temporal Lobe

Primary visual cortex

Primary auditory area

Cerebellum

Auditory association area

Fig. 30
Functional Areas of the Brain

peripheral nervous system, while the brain and spinal chord together are referred to as the central nervous system. This division of the nervous system into central and peripheral nervous systems is further characterized by the built in protection features. Physically, the central nervous system is protected by being encased in the bone of skull and spine, and toxicologically by the blood/brain barrier. The peripheral nervous system lacks these protections.

The division of the peripheral nervous system into sensory and motor nervous systems is based on the nature and direction of the neural streams: the sensory stream goes from the periphery to the center and the motor stream goes from the center to the periphery. We will examine the various aspects of the neural motor stream first, then those of the sensory neural stream, and finally their interface in the central nervous system.

The longitudinal axis of the human central nervous system physically recapitulates the spectrum of movement possibilities that evolved over time. There are three streams of motor activity that can activate the machinery of movement.

As defined by their neural origin, these streams represent different levels of evolutionary development. The lowest and highest of these levels are the basis for the division of the nervous system into the voluntary and involuntary (autonomic) nervous systems that each have their own set of neurons to activate the body's musculature.

The gamma neurons originate in the lower and more primitive levels of neural organization of the spinal chord, brainstem and cerebellum. They are primarily responsible for the muscular contraction involved in involuntary movements, such as simple or conditioned reflexes. They also are responsible for preserving levels of muscle tone and changes in muscle length that are the basis for inherited postural and movement reflexes.

Alpha neurons originate in the frontal motor cortex, the most highly evolved level of neural organization that allows self awareness and voluntary movement. Any voluntary act or intention produces a neural stimulus that sends signals through the alpha neurons down the spinal cord and out to the skeletal musculature to "tell" it to contract and produce movement such as "raise right arm." We will see how for internal martial arts theory and practice, the further distinction between initiative and responsive voluntary movement is extremely important.

Fixed Action Patterns

Between the extremes of totally involuntary and totally voluntary movement, there is a third type of movement that is indispensable in our set of movement skills. Since the day we were born, we have been busy learning movement patterns from all the people that constitute our human environment. Modern day neuroscientists have labelled such movement patterns faps, which as explained previously is the acronym for fixed action patterns.[40] From birth, we have been storing these faps in the giant library of movement memory files that resides in the basal ganglia of the brainstem and midbrain (Fig. 31).

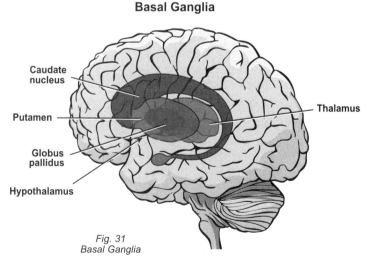

Basal Ganglia

Caudate nucleus

Putamen

Globus pallidus

Hypothalamus

Thalamus

Fig. 31
Basal Ganglia

[40] Rodolfo R. Llinas, "*i of the Vortex, From Neurons to Self, A Bradford Book,*" The MIT Press, Massachusetts, 2001, p. 133-4.

From here the faps can be activated or liberated to run, as the case may be, again and again at the appropriate time, which is when the right sensory stimulus occurs.

While more complex and elaborate than simple reflexes, faps can vary from relatively simple behaviors such as standing and walking to the very complex ones used in talking, athletic feats of prowess (think skateboarders, gymnasts, dancers, martial artists), and artistic mastery (a musician playing a difficult piece of music from memory or a master carver at work, etc.). All these behaviors involve faps, the ready made "motor tapes" that produce well-defined and coordinated movements when switched on. Faps in mammalian and primate history mainly evolved to respond selectively to events in the external world. Consequently, most are based on well-defined, overt strategies to deal with specific situations, such as attack or defense, finding food, reproduction, and the like, in a timely and appropriate fashion.[41]

The internal martial arts, also, are all about learning new faps, that is, acquiring new habits of posture and movement that derive their meaning from a larger context of strategies for defense and offense, and training until they become habitual. As we will see, in the internal martial arts, faps used for aligning the body's posture and its way of moving are designed to produce a certain internal realization of the body as a cohering unity of parts. Posture and movement take on the characteristics of a "smart" trampoline sphere that is as stable as it is agile, capable both of absorbing an opponent's energy and issuing jin, the spherically explosive force.

Sensory-Motor Integration in the Cerebral Cortex

The brain part of the central nervous system is constantly modeling, or mapping, external reality in order for it to be able to guide/control/direct the body's voluntary movements successfully. This modeling includes all three dimensions of space as well as the three aspects of time (past, present and future). The central nervous system takes present perceptions, compares them with past perceptions (memory) and associated past motor actions (faps), and comes to a conclusion about what's likely to happen in the future, and on that basis initiates and executes the body's voluntary movements.

---

[41] Ibid, p. 145.

The two most obvious structures of the brain involved in this mapping are the cerebrum, or neocortex, and the cerebellum. The perception of the external world and our voluntary movement in it are so intimately intertwined that they are jointly processed by the cerebrum. The cerebellum is specialized to process the internal senses of balance and proprioception. The cerebrum and cerebellum are uniquely interconnected and are in constant instantaneous communication. Together they integrate the data from the external and internal sensory streams, respectively, and that combined sensory awareness is the basis for deciding on and executing the voluntary movements originating in the frontal lobes.

The sensory-motor polarity is evident in the functional division of labor between the front and back areas of the neocortex. Separated from each other by a deep fissure called the central sulcus, the area in front of the sulcus is dedicated to processing the output of voluntary motor behavior, and the area in back of the sulcus towards the back of the brain is dedicated to processing the input of sensory data. Incoming sensory and outgoing motor neural streams are mirror images of each other. The incoming perceptual stream goes through three stages/areas from the concrete perceptions to highly abstract representations in the frontal lobe. The outgoing stream of motor impulses goes through three stages/areas from highly abstract intentions in the frontal lobe to concrete manifestation of physical movement.

The incoming streams of sensory data into the central nervous system are of two kinds: streams from the external senses (sight, sound, smell, taste, touch) and streams from the internal senses (balance and proprioception). The former are routed to the cerebrum, or neocortex, for processing, while the latter stream is routed to the cerebellum. Five primary receptor areas are dedicated to receive raw, unprocessed input directly from each of the senses and assemble that data into rough, preliminary perceptions. We will limit ourselves to exploring those that particularly relate to the internal martial arts. The occipital lobe processes visual data from the eyes; the temporal lobe processes sound data from the ears, the sensory cortex processes the tactile data from the body. From their primary areas these rough preliminary perceptions then travel to the sense specific secondary receptive areas where they are further refined and abstracted.

Next, the sensory perceptions move to the association areas, where the most sophisticated processing occurs; here sense stimuli gather together or "associate" with the neural information from various other parts of the brain. Of particular interest to the internal martial artist are the orientation association area localized in the parietal lobes and the attention association area localized in the frontal lobes. As the name indicates, the function of the parietal lobe's "orientation association area" is to orient us in our surrounding space. It is concerned with defining the outer boundaries of the self and the self's location relative to the objects in its immediately surrounding space. Both are issues of great relevance to the internal martial artist, as we will see.

On the motor side of the sensory-motor equation, the functions of the attention association area of the frontal lobes are also of intense interest to the internal martial artist. This is where attention becomes intention, and the outgoing stream of voluntary motor impulses originate. Here perception and awareness of the combined senses merge to mobilize the mechanics of movement into a course of action. The flow of motor impulses that results from the decision to engage in a voluntary behavior (i.e., movement) starts out at a highly abstract level. The initial impulse of intent is like a ballistic approximation aimed at the intended result that will be fine tuned along its way toward physical expression.

This fine tuning of intentional movement occurs in the secondary motor centers called the supplementary motor area and the pre-motor cortex. The supplementary motor area takes the prefrontal urge to move and concretizes it into a plan of action. By integrating it with other sensory data (tactile, kinesthetic, vestibular, or visual) from the periphery, the supplementary motor area refines a movement as it is being executed. Finally, the pre-motor cortex plans the details of the proposed motor activity and then sends the exact instructions to the primary motor cortex, which in turns activates the appropriate groups of muscles.

The Cerebellum: Integrating the Internal Senses

The cerebellum's primary function is to process the neural stream of internal sensory data pertaining to balance and proprioception, that is, the perception of the body's parts relative to each other. The cerebellum uses this information to facilitate the execution of the commands from the neocortex, and integrates conscious, voluntary movement with subconscious involuntary movement. In other words, in the cerebellum the alpha neurons from the neocortex, i.e., those that convey conscious will and volitional movement, interconnect and integrate with the subcortical gamma neurons from the spine and other points of origin, i.e., those that carry subconscious information pertaining to balance and proprioception.

Assessing its role in voluntary movement, we can say the cerebellum specializes in the execution of complicated but routine actions involving fine motor movement involved in standing, walking and other everyday life activities, namely the fixed actions patterns, or faps, discussed previously. The cerebellum integrates the gamma and alpha motor systems with each other and with sensory information gathered by all the senses, including sight, sound, and touch.[42] The cerebellum compares, in a manner of speaking, what you thought you were going to do (according to the motor cortex) with what is actually happening down in the limbs (according to proprioceptive feedback), and corrects and fine tunes the movement if there are any problems. When a person picks up a glass, for example, it is the cerebellum that controls the amount of pressure in the muscles in the hand so that the glass is not shattered or dropped.

These insights into the structure and functioning of the cerebellum also provide a new conceptual framework of interpretation and understanding of strategy in the internal martial arts. In particular, standing mediation profoundly changes the very relationship between the neocortex and cerebellum. Ordinarily, the frontal cortex remains unaware of the cerebellum's contributions to the realization of its wishes or commands, namely the data on balance and proprioception, or self-perception of one's parts relative to each other in posture and movement.

---

[42] Deane Juhan, op.cit., pp. 235-243.

Now, as we have stressed previously, the major philosophical and strategic tenet of the internal martial arts is that cultivating awareness of and control over our internal environment, namely, the self-perception of the whole (body) around its central equilibrium, gives us greater control over the external environment, namely, our opponents. And indeed, in standing meditation, more than anything else, it is the functions of the cerebellum, balance and proprioception, that become the very objects of frontal lobe attention and awareness.

From this point of view, it is not far fetched to conclude that in as much as the adoption of the upright bipedal posture was of pivotal importance in human evolution, by making conscious the cerebellum's unconscious functions of balance and proprioception, standing meditation becomes nothing less than the conscious pursuit of evolution.

Bilateral Cortical Asymmetry

The next structural feature of the brain's neural organization of interest to the internal martial artist is the bilateral division of the cortex into the left and right cortical hemispheres. A thick bundles of nerves called the corpus collussum connects these two hemispheres and allows instantaneous communication and integration between them.

The structure of the brain's left and right cortical hemispheres manifests the polarity principle at work in the brain's spatial organization in surprising ways. First, the left side of the brain processes what the right side perceives and instructs the right side how to move, and conversely, the right side of the brain processes what the left side perceives and instructs the left side how to move.

Second, there is a functional division of labor between the two hemispheres that defines the relationship between them as that of the complimentary halves of a whole. This dual interpenetrating awareness, astoundingly, generates a single seamless perception of the world. The principal division of labor between them is the following: whereas the left hemisphere looks at the parts of the whole, the right hemisphere looks at the whole of the parts.

Another way of expressing it is that the left occupies itself with the foreground or focus, while the right maps the background, or field, of any perceptual situation. For the internal martial artist this is of interest. The ability to shift instantaneously from a hard focus on detail to a soft focus that perceives the whole indicates a high level of hemispheric integration and defines the best martial artists.

Homo sapiens underwent a further evolutionary development of left-right hemispheric asymmetrical specialization of the neocortex. In humans, the temporal lobe of the left hemisphere, which handles hearing and smell in other mammals, evolved to handle the intricacies of language, conceptual thinking and consciousness. This left hemispheric specialization of the cerebral cortex also has important implications for the internal martial arts theory and training practices. Practically speaking, right hemispheric abilities are of greater value than left hemispheric abilities for the internal martial artist. Left hemispheric ability for abstract analysis may serve well before or after an internal martial arts engagement, to strategize and analyze. But during an engagement, as with any other sport, those left hemispheric skills are better left alone and kept quiet. Since if allowed to interfere, they will only guarantee disaster. Instead we must learn to rely on our right hemispheric abilities to guide our awareness because they are more directly linked to our sensory-motor processes.

Sympathetic and Parasympathetic Branches of the Nervous System: Energy Expenditure and Restoration

The division of the involuntary or autonomic nervous system into its sympathetic and parasympathetic constituents is based on the fundamental differences between the gathering or accumulation of biological energy, on the one hand, and the disposition or expenditure of it in movement on the other. Baseline human existence alternates between relative stillness and movement. The body is designed to move, but it can only move so much and for so long; then it must rest. In other words, under normal circumstances the sympathetic and parasympathetic branches operate in complementary fashion, where the activation of one entails the deactivation of the other.

The parasympathetic, or quiescent, system operates during the periods of stillness in daily life to cultivate and store energy. It optimizes and regulates the vegetative functions of digestion, reproduction, circulation, and respiration, and because it governs the charging phase, it is slower working. This system operates when a person is resting, eating, sleeping, and generally, relaxed and in balance. The sympathetic, or arousal, system is designed to expend energy in movement and other muscular exertion. Because the sympathetic system, in concert with the endocrine system, can activate the musculature very fast, it is also at the very core of our crisis response system.

As a crisis oriented response system, the sympathetic system itself is further sub-divided along the lines of the flight-fight polarity. Flight and fight represent the organism's two main strategies for survival when threatened: either disengage and get away from the threat, or engage it in order to incapacitate it. Many, if not most, of our innate and learned behavioral patterns, reflexes and faps, evolved to facilitate either flight or fight behavior. Whether for flight or for fight, sympathetic stimulation marshals the body's accumulated energy enabling the muscles to move the body faster and stronger to execute the relevant faps.

The relevance of the sympathetic-parasympathetic division of the autonomic nervous system to internal martial arts is profound. Internal martial arts training aspires to overide the sympathetic system so that it ceases to initiate and empower innate or previously learned fight or flight faps in crisis situations. Through the method of standing meditation training, the internal martial arts seek to replace all such faps with different ones, the faps that standing mediation develops to regulate body posture and movement. Because they are powered by the para-sympathetic system, these internal martial arts faps require far less expenditure of energy, increase perceptual awareness and are also capable of fajin, the explosive, whole-body force.

Part 3
On Yi

Developing the Mind to Control Power

Chapter 6: Yi as Neurological Interface

Yi as Polarity Structure

The Yang family's prowess in the art of taijiquan is legendary, attested to in numerous stories recounting both their power and responsiveness skills. One tale recounts founder Yang Luchan's (楊露禪, 1779-1872) mastery of fajin.[43] The story goes that while in Beijin, he was visited by a tall and powerfully built monk. The monk made his opening remarks in a humble and deferential manner, professing his admiration. But when Master Yang started in on his reply, all of a sudden the monk attacked him with great ferocity. Master Yang, hardly moving, and with what appeared to be only a casual shrug, sent the monk flying back as if struck by lighting. It took the monk a long time to get up (Fig. 32).

Fig. 32
The Master Bouncing the Monk

Another story about Yang Luchan illustrates equal mastery in responsiveness skills. Yang Luchan could hold a bird on his outstretched hand and the bird would be unable to fly away.[44] How could this be? To achieve flight, the bird had to push off with its legs and feet from the master's palm. But when it tried to do so, the master would yield minutely with the muscles of his palm, and the bird could not push off. The story evidences an extreme tactile sensitivity coupled with unbelievable motor responsiveness (Fig. 33). As the classics describe it elsewhere, this is a sensitivity so keen that not even a fly can land on one who has achieved mastery.

Fig. 33
Bird in Hand

---

[43] Douglas Wile, T'ai-chi Touchstones, op. cit., p. 100.

[44] Ibid, p. 101.

These two stories about Yang Luchan illustrate the polar nature of the yi, the mental faculty that directs our actions in the world. Parts 1 and 2 make frequent use of the phrase "making the involuntary voluntary." And indeed, the realm of the yi is the realm of the voluntary. The yi is first and foremost our decision-making agency, the instrument of assessment and intervention in the world.

For example, your very first decision to practice internal martial arts was a function of the yi. Likewise every time you decide to practice, it is a function of the yi. Each time you remind yourself to maintain proper posture and move according to the principles, each time you are mindful of your breathing or your muscular exertion, each time you perform fajin or do any of the associated activities discussed in Parts 1 and 2—all such choices and decisions are made and sustained by the yi. The yi directs the body to engage in the necessary, repetitive training until it restructures our posture and movement and becomes part of our default motor skill set.

While yi is often translated as either mind or intent, these terms are not equivalent.[45] Intention is a function of mind, but it is not the only one. For example, to be successful, any intention to intervene in the world must be based on attention, which is also a function of mind. Attention and intention are dual aspects of a common core of meaning. *Attention* is defined as "the concentrated direction of the mental powers," and *intention* as an "ultimate or immediate purpose or goal." The Latin root of both attention and intention is *tendere*, broadly meaning "to stretch."[46]

---

[45] Besides being translated as "intent", yi (意) is also sometimes translated as "will." However, as Louis Swaim pointed out to me (personal communication, 10/15/2011), although their meanings intersect, intent and will are not synonymous. "Will" is more appropriate as a translation of zhi (志) than of yi. What is the difference? Zhi is more cognitive and independent of the external world, and often involves long range thinking, as in ambition or the pursuit of an ideal. Yi, on the other hand, deals more with the immediacy of the present moment, and for that reason is more dependent on feedback from the senses. For example, a conscious decision to pursue the mastery of the internal martial arts knowing in advance that it might take a life time to accomplish, if ever, and the determination to stick to the practice when tempted to slack off, would be acts of will (power), zhi. On the other hand, during martial engagements, such as fighting or pushing hands, where the intent and the senses must function seamlessly together, it would be yi that is involved.

[46] Eirc Partridge, "*Origins, A Short Eytymological Dictionary of English*", The MacMillan Company, New York, 1958, p. 704.

Attention refers to a stretching or reaching with the mind's perceptual apparatus towards something merely to observe it; it is perceptual activity and passive in the motor sense. *Intention*, on the other hand, refers to stretching or reaching with the mind toward something with a plan or goal to affect it. In other words, intention activates the motor component. For this reason, yi must be thought of as a polarity structure, where the yin and the yang poles are attention and intention, which in partnership direct our actions in the world.

In voluntary movement, there is a yin-yang structure that echoes the polarity of the yi, namely the dynamic between initiative, intentional movement and responsive, attentional movement. Examples are a blind person being guided by a sighted person and one person leading while another follows in dancing. In both cases, leading is initiative movement, while following is responsive movement. In the internal martial arts, likewise, offensive movements are initiative while defensive movements are responsive. The story of Yang Luchan bouncing his opponent multiple feet away illustrates the yang aspect of the yi, the training of the intention to produce the fajin power. The story of Yang Luchan holding a bird in his hand illustrates the yin aspect of the yi, the training of the attention and responsiveness skills. This difference between initiative movement, based on intention, and responsive movement, based on attention, is also the cornerstone of internal martial arts philosophy, strategy, training theory and practice.

The yi, as the neural nexus, or interface, of attention and intention is largely localized in the brain's frontal lobes, particularly in that part of the cortex known as the attention association area, or AAA. It is in the AAA that the focus of perceptual attention becomes the spark of intent that initiates a voluntary motor response ranging from the very simple to the very complex. In humans, moreover, the functions of the AAA have evolved to the point that they transcend mere motor functions and become involved in many other types of goal-oriented behavior, including the purposeful organization of thought itself.

Let us begin by following the path of a tactile stimulus from skin to the brain, and then outline the stages that stimulus goes through as the brain processes and transforms it into a voluntary motor response.

From Tactile Stimulus to Motor Response

The internal martial arts are contact sports. Therefore, to refine our understanding and practice, it is important to understand the physiology and the psychology of touch and pressure. Watching for the first time a master's response to an attack leaves one wondering, "What just happened?" As the story of Master Yang relates, at the lightest touch the master throws the opponent back with no apparent use of force. There is an ancient internal martial arts saying: "Once they touch, they go." For those unacquainted with the internal martial arts, and sometimes even to long-time students, it seems inexplicable, almost a sort of magic. How can it be possible?

Our journey to understanding begins with a simple thought experiment. *Imagine one person, call him Jack, holding up his arm and another person, call her Jill, in the process of putting a palm on Jack's forearm. (For now, we will assume the two people are not trained in internal martial arts methods. This will give us a foundation for later discussion about differences in perception and response between two skilled internal martial artists.) Initially, even before Jill's hand touches Jack's skin the current of air preceding her approaching hand interacts with the hairs of Jack's arms. The hair being moved by air activates what is properly called the "hair-end organ," the nerve-ending sensor that allows us to pick up sensations of near objects before they even touch our skin.*

When Jill's hand actually touches Jack's skin, some specialized sensors in the superficial tissue layers underneath the skin detect those light and fleeting touch sensations. Others sensors are specialized to differentiate long, continuing signals from more constant pressures. A similar division of labor exists in deeper tissue layers where heavier pressures are experienced: Pacinian corpuscles detect rapid distortions, fleeting pressures, and vibrations, while specialized sensors called Ruffini organs detect sustained pressure.

In the body's ongoing endeavor to maintain posture and produce accurate movement in space, the Pacinian corpuscles and Ruffini organs (particularly abundant in all joint capsules where all limb adjustments occur) act in partnership with the Golgi organs (abundant in the tendons where they sense the stresses on the tendons and other connective tissue), and the muscle spindles (that measure the individual and collective exertions of the muscle fibers).

Of course many instances of people touching each other involve light, accidental pressure and the adjustments on the part of the recipient frequently are automatic and below the level of conscious awareness. When this is the case, the different parameters of the tactile data, such as force, direction, intensity and duration, provided by all the specialized tactile receptors, are delivered to the cerebellum for integration and involuntary reflex management.

The greater the pressure exerted by Jill, the more it will impinge on Jack's awareness and become the focus of his attention. Moreover, the greater the pressure Jack experiences, the more his body has to adjust behind the point of contact in order to maintain position. Lastly, the stronger the pressure exerted by Jill, the more likely Jack will interpret it as an intentional challenge that requires a considered response on his part. In this latter situation, when Jack's efforts to maintain postural integrity and movement control occur on a conscious level, the data regarding touch and pressure from all the specialized tactile receptors (the Pacinian corpuscles, Rufinni organs, Golgi organs and muscles spindles) are delivered not only to his cerebellum for subconscious integration, but also to his sensory cortex as the first step towards voluntary response management.

The neural pathways of the sensory and motor data mirror each other in structure and function. They each have primary, secondary, and tertiary centers of information processing. The flow of neural traffic, however, is reversed. In the situation described above, neural data from Jack's sense of touch flow inward toward his AAA (attention association area) and the motor pathways flow outward away from the AAA towards their target muscles. The sensory processing begins at the primary center, the sensory cortex, with raw pattern perception. Augmented in the secondary center, the perceived patterns then ascend to be refined into highly abstract representations in the AAA. The motor flow starts in the AAA at a highly abstract level of mapping, is made into a more concrete plan in the supplementary motor area and finally the primary motor cortex sends the specific instruction out to the muscles in the body.

Jack's sensory cortex is the initial processing area where tactile stimuli begin their transformation into attentional awareness. Physically, the sensory cortex covers the mid-section of the upper surface of the brain in front of the post-central gyrus of the cerebral cortex. Here the raw, unprocessed input from the touch and pressure receptors is assembled into rough, preliminary perceptions. In the process, a strict one-to-one relationship is maintained between the parts of the sensory cortex and the corresponding areas of the skin and body. As Deane Juhan, the philosopher of bodywork, has written so aptly: "The skin is the surface of the brain." The pressure of Jill's hand on Jack's arm is felt in the corresponding spot of Jack's sensory cortex. For that reason, the sensory cortex, and its twin counterpart the motor cortex, are called "projection" areas. Together they take up 25 percent of the available space of the cortex.

The final destination of sensory (in this case, tactile) input is the AAA of Jack's prefrontal lobe. Association areas are so called because that's where sense stimuli are gathered together, to "associate" with the neural information from other parts of the brain and flesh out the totality of the sensation. For example, in the "orientation association areas" of Jack's parietal lobes, the tactile data of the sensory cortex associates and interacts with optical data from the occipital lobe to complete the mapping of our selves and our opponent in the three-dimensional space of the external environment. This parietal data, along with processed data from the sensory cortex and cerebellum, is shared and connected with the AAA in Jack's pre-frontal cortex for final integration by the yi in its process of making a voluntary, intentional act in response to the provocation.

Now Jill slowly begins to increase the intensity (pressure) of her touch pressure on Jack's arm. Her force becomes more insistent, almost provocative. As a result, the point of contact moves from being on the fringes of Jack's awareness to the center of his attention. And as Jack's discomfort with the situation increases, a desire to do something about it fuels the active preparation of his body. The yi, in other words, is aroused into a consideration of possible alternative responses. Jack, for example, might consider the purely verbal approach and ask Jill to stop. Or Jack could withdraw his arm voluntarily to relieve the pressure and let it go at that. Or perhaps to show his discontent, he could consider turning around in a huff and walking away. Or more assertively, he might be tempted to push back against the pressure. Or Jack might envision an even more direct "don't mess with me" signal such as grabbing Jill's arm or slapping it away.

All the various scenarios are run through the memory banks and compared by Jack's yi to previous, similar situations along with whatever responses were used to resolve the situation successfully. Equally important is the emotional component of the yi's decision in selecting one of the options as the most appropriate one and then issuing the orders to the muscles to execute it. After brief reflection, Jack decides the wiser course is to take the more restrained action and he simply withdraws his arm to relieve the pressure and regain a more acceptable balance.

The decision by Jack's yi that eventually results in a flow of motor impulses to withdraw his arm starts out at a highly abstract level in his AAA. The initial intent results in a crude motor impulse that is fine-tuned as the signals move through secondary motor centers called the supplementary motor area and the pre-motor cortex. Jack's supplementary motor area takes the prefrontal urge to remove the hand and makes the plan of action concrete, integrating it with other sensory data (tactile, kinesthetic, vestibular and visual) to refine the movement as it is being executed. Next, Jack's pre-motor cortex plans the details of the proposed motor activity and sends the exact instructions to the primary motor cortex, which in turn activates the appropriate groups of muscles.

The contribution of Jack's cerebellum to this process of producing voluntary movement cannot be overestimated. The feedback loops between cerebellum and cerebral cortex continually modify ongoing motor commands, constantly refining them in the light of the most current sensory information. In the final few hundred milliseconds before completing the voluntary withdrawal of Jack's arm ordered by his yi, his cerebellum uses its knowledge about the internal states pertaining to equilibrium, postural reflexes and muscle tone to smooth the execution of the movement plan. Lastly, the flow of neural impulses from the pre-motor cortex and the adjustments by the cerebellum meet up on the primary motor cortex map, located towards the back of the frontal lobe. Jack's cerebellum in turn activates the appropriate groups of muscles to create the intended movement of withdrawing his arm to release the pressure exerted by Jill's hand.

Use of the Yi in Internal Martial Arts

For purposes of illustration, the interaction between Jack and Jill described above was set up in the manner of a laboratory type experiment. Jill increased the pressure on Jack's hand slowly and gradually, making Jack aware of the entire process as it was taking place. Slowly Jack was forced into the position where he felt he had to do something about Jill's overly insistent familiarity. In reality of course, most tactile interactions between people are likely to be more accidental than intentional and more abrupt than sustained.

But of course, a tactile encounter can be both intentional and abrupt. Imagine how Jack might react if Jill changed the rules and suddenly attacked him, pushing hard and sharp at the point of contact on his arm. If Jack was untrained, that would most likely be the end of any voluntary response. Instead, his limbic system would immediately declare a crisis and intervene. Attention would contract in sharp focus on the perceived threat as part as the body's general preparation and set off a chain of involuntary, reflexive reactions—some combination of startle, withdrawal or resistance, fight or flight.

And how would it be different if Jack was a trained internal martial artist? A sudden attack by Jill would certainly constitute an acid test of how effectively Jack's training had reprogrammed the integration between his sensory and motor systems. The ability to not react reflexively and involuntarily, but to respond with awareness no matter how swiftly and forcefully the parameters of the touch are changing, is a defining characteristic of internal martial arts mastery.

Take Master Tam, for example. Countless are the times I've seen folks attempt something like Jill's sudden attack on Jack. In all those times, I've never seen Master Tam startle or exhibit any involuntary, reflexive reaction. Rather, upon being touched—whether suddenly or slowly, softly or hard—Master Tam calmly disables and disarms his opponent by connecting with and capturing his opponent's center.

How and why? Master Tam perceives, feels and treats any tactile stimulus, no matter how light the pressure, as constituting a direct line of force connecting his own center physically to that of his opponent. By skillfully controlling this connection, and before ever using or applying any force himself, Master Tam takes control over his opponent's balance and hijacks it. In fact, even before an opponent ever makes contact, Master Tam has that person's number. My own experience is illustrative. I remember once while touching only the hair on Master Tam's arm, I realized I was unable to reach further and touch his skin. Nor was I able to move away from him and lose touch with the hair. How could this be? One of the predictable results of standing meditation is that the increased circulation of the blood and qi will open the pores in the skin which in turn makes the hairs stand erect,[47] increasing their reach and sensitivity to the slightest pressure stimuli. Grandmaster Wang Xiangzhai peppered his writings with references to the phenomenon of the body hair standing straight up: "the hairs should bristle"[48]; "the hairs (are) standing as a forest"[49]; "the hairs (shot up) like halberds (ji 戟)."[50]

So keen is Master Tam's ability to follow and stick that where my fingers touched the hair on his arm I felt as though I was touching a piece of scotch tape. No matter what I did, I was unable to get rid of that scotch tape. I was neither able to increase or decrease the distance from my fingertips to his arm—a hair's length, literally about a quarter-inch, separated us. It occurred to me later that the bird in Yang Luchan's hand must have felt that way when it was trying to fly away but could not.

Master Tam demonstrates the truth of the ancient warrior's maxim, "I know my opponent, but he does not know me." Everytime an opponent makes contact with him, Master Tam, is immediately tuned into the strength and weaknesses of his opponent's central equilibrium and is fully aware of that person's balance. The opponent, however, has no clue either about her own center or balance, or about Master Tam's.

How can this be? The answer is in the use of the unique combination of physical and mental readiness skills developed through standing meditation practice. Physically, Master Tam always has his frame at the ready, there is no time lost activating it when he needs it. Mentally, Master Tam's perceptual awareness is habitually whole and never

---

[47] Wang Xiangzhai, "*The Right Path of Yiquan*," op.cit., p. 16.

[48] Wang Xiangzhai, "*The Essence of Martial Art: The Theory of Yiquan*," op.cit., p.18.

[49] Ibid, p. 23.

[50] Ibid, p. 32.

partial; because it is always present, there is no time wasted shifting the focus of attention from one thing to another. Thus Master Tam's response time approaches true simultaneity with the stimulus.

In the final analysis, Master Tam's is able to capture his opponent's center because his own yi, in both its attentive and intentional functions, is so finely attuned to his opponent that he is capable of working below his opponent's threshold of perception. His opponent doesn't stand a chance. Responding to stimuli in real time, Master Tam's yi instantaneously and simultaneously adjusts to changing touch and pressure. By adjusting the tension of the connective tissue web and his elastic body frame, Master Tam can make his opponents pay in a variety of ways, all of which are completely involuntary and, consequently, seem totally bewildering to them.

For example, the moment you try to use force on Master Tam's arm in the manner of Jill pushing on Jack, you may find yourself nailed down to the floor, seemingly paralyzed and completely unable to move. Or by freezing his frame into total solidity, Master Tam may instantaneously shoot your own energy back into you, causing you to stiffen involuntarely and bounce back as if you had hit a wall. Or he may choose to go the opposite route and the moment you exert force on him, the solid target you expected will not be there and you will land on emptiness, your momentum causing you to loose balance, as if falling into a sudden hole. Or he may accept your force and move with it, yielding to your force in a circular fashion to capture your center, and on the return use your own force to bounce you backward like a rock lauched by a slingshot.

...

The yi stage is often described as consisting of the mastery of the purely mental control of jin, meaning the direct intentional use of the diaphragm and spine to issue the power of the whole-body reflex. Thought of this way, the yi stage indeed represents a higher level than the jin stage: the jin (power) issued directly by the yi is faster and more dangerous than the jin issued indirectly by the yi, which uses reverse breathing to activate the chi.

From the point of view being developed in this chapter and the next, however, the commonly held idea, expressed above, is still incomplete and too narrow. It does not reflect the polarity structure that is the essence of the yi. It only expresses the the yang side of the yi , i.e., the skills of intention and physical power. It neglects to incorporate the yin side of the yi, namely, the perceptual attention on which any intention is based.

For the truth is that any muscular effort generated by intention can only be as susccessful as the accuracy of the perceptual attention on which it was based. Indeed, in the final analysis, as we will see in the next chapter, the attention-based skills that lead to superior motor responsiveness not only are the prerequisite for intentional acts generally, but in the internal martial arts they also are the only antidote for fajin, the skill of explosive power (jin) based on intention.

Chapter 7: From Reaction to Response

The Time it Takes to Move

In sports, as in life, timing is everything. Excellence in athletic performance is achieved when players, by virtue of their natural endowment and their training regimen, are able to push the limits of their responsiveness. Particularly in game sports, where the difference between winning and losing is often a split second or a fraction of an inch, the ability of athletes to modify planned actions in real time so as to coincide with the changing situations of the game is often what distinguishes great players from merely good ones.

In the martial arts, the level of sensory-motor integration achieved by the yi is the main factor in high-level mastery of timing. Moreover, response times in the martial arts vary according to the type of stimulus involved, whether visual, auditory or tactile. In the external martial arts, because they are primarily long-distance fighting systems that launch their punches and kicks like projectiles towards their opponents, most of the clues and stimuli are visual. The internal martial arts, on the other hand, are close-in fighting systems, and tactile sensations of pressure are of major import.

In the internal martial arts, Master Tam differentiates between reaction and response on the basis of both time and awareness. A reaction always occurs after the stimulus, whereas a response occurs simultaneously with the stimulus. Neurologically, a reaction is an automatic and involuntary event, either a spinal reflex or a sub-cortical fixed action pattern, with a time delay between the sensory input and the subsequent behavior it generates. A response, on the other hand, is voluntary, generated in the cortex. In fact, it is precisely the awareness that makes possible the simultaneity of stimulus and response.

The quickest automatic reflex action of which a human is capable is about one-tenth of a second, or 100 milliseconds. For example, in athletic races, that's the time it takes runners to respond to the crack of a starter's pistol and begin moving forward. For the wide range of more complex movement patterns that reside in the basal ganglia, it takes a minimum of 200 milliseconds to make a correction to an unanticipated change.[51] This is the same as the minimum amount of time that elapses between the stimulus and reaction in the startle reflex, in which a person's entire emotional and physical state is reset to optimize it for the moment ahead. Of course, the more complex the stimulus, the longer mind and body take to reset and reorient.

When we investigate the speed of voluntary movement, we quickly come to the realization that paradoxically, voluntary movement is both the fastest and the slowest kind of movement in which we engage. Initiative movement based on intention produces the slowest kind of movement; the responsive movement based on attention is the fastest. This has deep and far-reaching implications for internal martial art theory, strategy and tactics.

The Time it Takes to Decide

Physicist Niels Bohr, the Nobel Prize winner who discovered the structure of the atom, was well-known to have a passion for American western movies. What intrigued him particularly was an apparent paradox: while the bad guy in black always is the first to draw, the good guy in white always is the one to fire first (Fig. 34). The man in black, the initiator, is consistently gunned down by the man in white, the responder.[52]

Fig. 34
Gunslinger Evidence:
The First Shall Be The Last

---

[51] Ibid, p. 143.

[52] Tor Norretranders, "*The User Illusion: Cutting Consciousness Down to Size,*" Viking, New York, NY, 1991, pp. 255-6.

This result was contrary to the expected result since, in a duel to the death where every fraction of a second counts, the first to draw would appear to have the clear advantage. So intrigued was Bohr by this seeming paradox that he enlisted fellow scientists to test the observation. In experiments they proved to their own satisfaction that the result was not just cinematic staging, but had a factual basis that makes it predictable and reproducible in real life.

The counterintuitive conclusion that Bohr and his colleagues were forced to accept as the truth was that any action, e.g., drawing the gun, is faster when done as an attentive response than when done as an initiative, or intentional, action. Bohr observed that the one who draws the gun first makes a decision to do so; it is an intentional act. On the other hand, the act of drawing by the responder is an automatic, conditioned response. He reasoned that the conscious volitional act, because of its complexity, takes a longer time to execute than an action that is purely conditional and requires no conscious thought or intention.

Bohr's conclusions dovetail exceedingly well with recent physiological and psychological research into the neurological mechanisms of thought and action. The psychologist Benjamin Libet corroborated Bohr's conclusion that the explanation for the phenomenon described exists in the differences between volitional acts and faps, the automatic fixed action patterns. More recently, a new study conducted at the University of Birmingham in the United Kingdom repeated Bohr's experiments and again corroborated his conclusions.[53]

Libet made this monumental discovery: there is a surprisingly long build-up, as much as half a second, of neural potential in the parts of the cortex responsible for motor control before an individual is able to execute a conscious movement.[54] That is 2.5 to 5 times slower than the 100-200 milliseconds it takes for simple reflexes and more complex faps to respond. This clear difference in the time it takes conscious, volitional action to complete a movement compared to conditioned response action (reflex), is literally the difference between life and death.

---

[53] BBC NEWS: 2010/02/03 07:26:33 GMT; http://news.bbc.co.uk/go/pr/fr/-/today/hi/today/newsid_8493000/8493203.stm

[54] McCrone, op. cit., p. 132.

In the stillness that precedes the gun fight, the man in black goes through a time-intensive decision-making process, a chain of reasoning and of weighing alternatives that leads finally to the decision to act. This decision-making process is communicated by subtle and involuntary cues which can be perceived by the trained observer—in this case, the man in white. In the stillness that precedes his fap response to the man in black, no conscious mental evaluative processes occur in the mind of the man in white. He only waits in readiness and then responds correctly.

The Strategy of Readiness

The implications of the gunfighters' face-off situation are profound and directly applicable to, and expressive of, internal martial arts theory and strategy. These turn completely upside-down the conventional wisdom that the best defense is a good offense. The internal martial arts stance, like the gunfighter's, is literally that *the best defense is to give no offense*, but in the meantime, to always be totally ready for someone else to initiate hostilities. The very essence of the standing meditation practice, after all, is being physically and mentally ready, that is, with full sensory–motor integration.

Philosophically speaking, waiting for the opponent to make the first move constitutes the moral high road. But in fortuitous coincidence, it also bestows a great strategic advantage to the internal martial artist. The internal martial artist considers the time difference between a conscious act of will and a fap response a crucial strategic advantage because the former takes a half-second longer than the latter. Hence the internal martial arts saying, often quoted by Master Tam: "You may start first, but I will finish it."

Understanding that "the fastest movement is no movement" is what allows the internal martial artist's defense response to become simultaneous to the offensive stimuli. Both as a matter of principle and as a matter of strategy, one always waits to let the opponent make the first move. Reading the decision-making process, one responds by moving with the opponent in the direction she wants to go without offering any resistance.

In this interval of interaction—between the opponent starting it and you finishing it—exists the dance where you must accept the opponent's lead and go where she wants to go. And while doing so, you must work below her threshold of perception to hijack her central equilibrium and render her helpless.

As opposed to the gun duelers where the stimuli are mostly visual, the stimuli that govern the responses of the internal martial artist are predominantly tactile, and must therefore be even more instantaneous and immediate, simultaneous with the changing stimuli. Since the internal martial arts are contact sports, the slightest change in intention is communicated at the point of contact. For example, the intention to attack can be sensed, and the body can simultaneously shift back and yield in response. Of course in doing so one must always keep in mind the maxim often quoted by Master Tam: "Only yield in order to get into a more advantageous position to attack."

For the internal martial artist to make the simultaneity of action and response the cornerstone of her skill set, she must eliminate the time that passes from receipt of the stimulus to the execution of the response. This eliminates both intention-based initiative action, with its half-second built in delay, and all spinal chord reflexes and faps stored in the basal ganglia which, no matter how fast, still involve a time lag between stimulus and response. That leaves real-time, attention-based responsiveness as the only option for action. Only awareness itself is capable of simultaneous adjustments of one's movement in response to changing pressures experienced at a given point of contact.

Key in developing the simultaneity of stimulus and response is the elastic frame developed in standing meditation by six directions training. The muscular effort of "mutual enervation and oppositional exertion" of agonist and antagonist muscles not only creates a dynamic tension between them, but also stretches their respective matrices of tendons, fascia and connective tissues. This results in near instantaneous communication and force transference between the agonist-antagonist pairings and is central to whole-body responsiveness training.

For example, it is easier and faster to reverse an action by going from 60 percent agonist/40 percent antagonist flexing to 40 percent agonist/60 percent antagonist extending than it is to go from 100 percent agonist/0 percent antagonist to 0 percent agonist/100 percent antagonist.

The simultaneity of stimulus and response is most succinctly expressed in the classic internal martial arts saying Master Tam likes to quote: "To yield is to attack." To help understand this maxim, it is useful to make the analogy of the human body's structure to a revolving door. When a person pushing a revolving door open doesn't step through quickly enough, she is hit from behind by the next blade of the revolving door, and loses balance. The internal martial artist's mastery of central equilibrium allows her to function much like a revolving door. When she is attacked on the right side, she simply yields by rotating her torso to the right, while using that very rotation to attack her opponent simultaneously with the left side of her body.

Countless are the times I have tried to push or attack Master Tam only to have him rotate an inch or even a quarter-inch to the right or left to deflect my force and connect with me on the opposite side. In that manner, he returns my own force to me and throws me off balance. Yielding on the right becomes an attack from the left, and vice versa.

The awareness training of our neuro-sensory apparatus and processes allows us not only to detect the decision-making process in our opponent, but to intervene with our own response before she has time to complete her decision-making process and issue the *go* command. Indeed, as mental tranquility deepens, it is possible to go beyond simultaneity and develop apparently pre-cognitive and telepathic (and therefore preemptive) abilities. Paradoxical as it sounds, Master Tam often knows what I am going to do before I do.

The Master's Touch

A stage magician's ability to produce an "impossible" card is attributable to the micro-movements of her hands below the threshold of perception while diverting the visual attention of the audience. One who experiences the skill of an internal martial artist may suddenly and inexplicably lose her balance, be frozen to the ground or find herself eight feet away without quite knowing how she got there, all for a similar reason: the internal martial artist works below the threshold of an opponent's perception to confuse the opponent's nervous system and capture the center.

Though I have both observed and experienced this many times, it is nonetheless difficult to convey the utter sense of bafflement that comes over one. At first it did seem supernatural, and I scratched my head for many years before I began to have an inkling that the key to unlocking this enigma lay in the logic of subtlety and the ranges of human perception. Since I can claim some real experience in being on the receiving end of Master Tam's skills, I feel rather well-qualified to offer a description and analysis of that experience. Observing the curious and hopeful who have received a personal education at the hands of Master Tam throughout the years, I've seen my own range of feelings and reactions mirrored hundreds of times.

According to the criteria described above, the skills of the internal martial artist certainly qualify as acts of magic. Like the stage magician, she works below the threshold of perception. But where the stage magician primarily works below the threshold of visual perception, the internal martial artist primarily works below the threshold of tactile perception. The sensation of trying to touch Master Tam when he doesn't want to be touched is like trying to catch the wind or get a grip on a glob of quicksilver. It simply can't be done. Other times, it may feel like pushing in on a spherical trampoline that absorbs all one's force and steals one's balance; then like a pebble in a slingshot that Master Tam merely has to decide when to shoot across the room. But understand: no matter what it feels like when you're touching him, whether feather-light, or elastic as rubber, or steel-hard, you are completely under his control. He can decide the course of action. And you, try as you might, can do nothing about it.

Engaging the Center

My "hands-on" familiarity with the process has led me to the conclusion that no matter of how brief the moment, there are four distinct aspects that describe the sequence of events leading to this experience. These components are:

1. **touching** the opponent
2. **connecting** with the opponent's center
3. **capturing** the opponent's center
4. **delivering fajin** to the opponent's center

Of course, it must be kept in mind that these aspects, though described as a sequence of events, in reality occur so fast as to be simultaneous. However, for educational and training purposes, it is extremely beneficial to isolate these aspects functionally and work on them separately. First we isolate the instant of touch, then we isolate the moment of connection, next we isolate the moment of capture, and finally we isolate the moment of delivery.

The usual martial arts mentality is to ignore the touching, connecting and capturing skills, and concentrate all effort on the skill of delivering the force. But in the internal martial arts, each aspect in the sequence is a prerequisite skill for the next. Working backward, we cannot deliver the force properly if we do not know how to capture the center.

We cannot capture the center unless we know how to connect with it. And we cannot connect with it, physically at least, unless we touch. Most importantly, we seek to isolate the skills of connecting and capturing from the skill of delivering the force. and come to appreciate them as an entirely separate sets of skills that require separate training regimens.

At first, then, touching precedes connecting. The situation described in the "The Path of a Tactile Stimulus" section in the last chapter is an example of touching without connecting; there is a collapsed physical structure and no mental awareness of any lines of force connecting the centers (Fig. 35). In

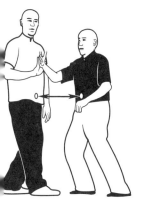

Fig. 35
Connecting with the Center

touching, you touch the skin or the outside periphery; in *connecting* you touch the internal center. By sinking your qi (relaxing to lower the center of gravity) and expanding your awareness from your center throughout your own frame, at the point of contact you connect, through your opponent's frame, with her center. Once you have developed the skill, touching and connecting become simultaneous. Connecting to the center is prerequisite to capturing it, but once the two centers are connected, each person has equal opportunity to capture the other's center.

The Moment of Joy

To capture an opponent's center means to cause her to lose balance. Master Tam explained once that in order to capture someone's center without force, "you must create a conflict between the conscious and subconscious parts of your opponent's mind." What he is able to do when he touches you is to bypass the level of your yi, or the conscious awareness of the cortex, while affecting the subconscious levels of the nervous system at the level of fixed action patterns stored in the basal ganglia and/or spinal reflexes. This means that on a conscious level, you have not noticed anything wrong, but on the reflexive level of the subconscious, the spinal part of the nervous system does perceive a danger and the body tightens in reflexive, involuntary tension.

Master Tam's most effective tool in this effort of creating a conflict between the conscious and subconscious parts of our minds is his ability to work far beneath the threshold of perception, both tactile and visual. His softness and lightness can operate far below my conscious perception, let alone the perception of danger, and therefore he can at will induce either loss of balance or startle reaction in me which causes me to tighten and create an involuntary frame. At that point he can manipulate me to his advantage—and my severe disadvantage.

The nervous system is a prediction machine. Based on past experience, it predicts what is going to happen in any given situation to enable the body to act appropriately. Master Tam's ability to work below his opponent's perceptual radar allows him to subvert the functioning of his opponent's nervous system as a prediction machine, and cause it to make the wrong predictions, thus creating further conflict between the conscious and subconscious components of the nervous system that the body/mind must address and resolve.

In other words, once you accept Master Tam's invitation to touch and try something and you reach out to do so, your nervous system begins making predictions about how and when things will happen. With the great ones like Master Tam, the wisdom underlying the classic advice becomes apparent: "Always let your opponent make the first move." Often times such masters present a seeming vulnerability, so that whatever opportunity you think you see, whatever you feel you can do, is really all a set-up. It's bait designed to lure you into a trap and when you bite and go for it, you're finished.

How does Master Tam use his yi to confound the predictions, conscious and subconscious, that his opponent's nervous system is making about the situation? He seems to have an infinite number of ways to do so at his disposal. Sometimes he uses the strategy of "not being there" or "only being there a little bit" and gives the opponent a point of contact, but because his yielding is exquisitely subtle, there is no possibility of using that point for the application of force.

And so the opponent is enticed to reach, and in reaching, she loses her balance. Sometimes Master Tam uses the opposite approach which may be called the strategy of "being there more," and gives his opponent a frame, thereby seeming to create an opening for the opponent to attack. Of course the moment one tries it, one lands on nothing and again loses balance. Sometimes Master Tam moves in so lightly towards his opponent's center that the opponent doesn't even notice it. But when all of a sudden the opponent's nervous system does register that the body's stability has been compromised, the opponent startles, stiffens, and again, loses.

Fig. 36
The Moment of Joy

Something that all of these scenarios have in common is that at the appropriate moment they create the mistaken belief in the opponent that Master Tam is inadvertently revealing a vulnerability that can be exploited. Master Tam, with clear delight, calls this set-up "giving them the moment of joy" (Fig. 36). Unfortunately, the "moment of joy" experience is inevitably followed by the "taste of death" experience. All of a sudden and most unexpectedly, with victory seemingly within reach, you find yourself paralyzed, powerless to move, and often in a very, very uncomfortable position.

The Taste of Death

With Master Tam, the moment of capture is a moment of supreme vulnerability for

his opponent–a moment when the opponent's mind and body are effectively paralyzed. Master Tam calls this moment jokingly, but very accurately, the "taste of death" (Fig. 37). By capture, as already discussed, we mean taking control over our opponent's center and balance, incapacitating her and rendering her helpless. The greater the awareness and the lighter the touch, the more imperceptible the frame behind it is. In turn, then, the more subtle the connection is, the more surprising and devastating the capture will be.

Fig. 37
The Taste of Death

Capture of the center must precede delivery of the jin, the explosive force. Why? If you attempt to deliver the force without having captured your opponent's center, the tables can be turned on you. But once you have captured your opponent's center and provoked her into an involuntary stiffening and integration of her frame, she is momentarily paralyzed; then it is safe to issue the jin. When Master Tam captures your center, he has complete and minutely calibrated control over how much force will be delivered. He may choose simply to let you lose balance, or he may nudge you slightly to guide your fall. Or he may just return the amount of force that you directed at him which he neutralized. Or he may add to it from his own stored energy.

Master Tam's ability to change the substance of his frame along a spectrum from very solid to very elastic also accounts for the different qualities he can impart to his jin. For example, he can issue jin as it is delivered by practitioners of taijiquan, xingyi, yiquan, bagua and other schools. At the most solid end of the spectrum, Master Tam becomes as firm and immobile as a wall. This "stand and deliver" mode illustrates, again, one of his favorite sayings, "Once they touch they go." Using the opponent's own force and without moving, Master Tam bounces the opponent back, instantaneously and immediately, or else crumples the opponent to the floor. However, when Master Tam allows his own frame to become more elastic, the time interval lengthens, both for absorbing the force and momentum of the incoming attack and for the invitable bounce-back. At this point the "attacker" becomes a projectile in a slingshot and is catapulted back in the direction from which she came, just as a trampoline absorbs the energy of the jumper's fall and shoots her back into the air.

Turning Enemies into Friends

The "taste of death" moment ends, usually, with a stay of execution. Mercifully, Master Tam usually gives you back no more than you put in. Occasionally, though, when a student is particularly hard of learning, I have observed Master Tam prolong the lesson just a bit, strictly for educational purposes, and sustain the "moment of death" experience by means of gentle, but excruciatingly unpleasant joint locks and pressure point paralysis.

As I wrote in the preface, the first time I touched Master Tam and he moved me, just inches, I was not only baffled, but a bit frustrated as well. I've since seen the same response hundreds of times in high-level martial artists from all over the world. When they're invited to touch him, they're curious, usually skeptical, sometimes even hostile, and then they reach toward his arm. As they engage, perhaps one sees the "moment of joy" register in their expressions, but then suddenly these challengers begin to look vaguely incredulous, as their centers are captured and gently they are incapacitated and paralyzed. Then the "taste of death" hits, as the realization dawns that they have been inexplicably disarmed, both physically and psychologically. Invariably, reluctant little smiles playing on their lips, they ask: "Would you do that again?"

Why the puzzlement? Why the slightly silly expressions? Why the head-scratching? Because they didn't feel anything! Without any warning, all of a sudden, they were no longer in control of their balance. The lightness of touch in the capture is Master Tam's signature. It is also the proof of his claim that while the external martial arts' interactive training tends to "make enemies out of our friends," the internal martial arts partnered training lets one "make friends out of our enemies" (Fig. 38). The "taste of death" experience demonstrates to the challenger unequivocally that Master

Fig. 38
Enemies into Friends

Tam can "finish" it, at any time and to any degree. So when he releases them gently and without causing harm, they are even more appreciative of his spirit and his skill.

Chapter 8: In The Laboratory of Responsiveness

The Name of the Game

The internal martial arts utilize a variety of partnered exercises that embody both general principles and specific techniques of conflict resolution, internal martial arts style. These exercises are the practical training laboratory and testing ground for both the yang (intention) and the yin (attention) of voluntary motor activity—on the one hand, the generation and delivery of jin, which we already discussed in Part 2 and, on the other, the awareness and responsiveness training. Thus, as we continue to explore the four-phase formula that we identified in the previous chapter–touch, connect, capture (the center), and deliver (the force)–our main concern here is to investigate the art of capturing the center in a more systematic way.

Various disciplines may refer to these exercises by different names. In Wing Tsun, for example, they are called chishou (黐手) or sticky hands, while in taiji and yiquan they are mostly called tuishou (推手). The meaning of tuishou is quite simply "pushing hands," a kind of nickname that early on became the popular way of referring to the activity, based no doubt, on the obvious interaction of the hands and arms.

Despite the simplicity of translation, there has been, from the beginning, resistance to the term's acceptance. When the first texts on internal martial arts were published in English in the 1970s, written mostly by Chinese writers such as Wen Shan Huang[55] and Yearning K. Chen,[56] the term tuishou was often rendered as "joint hand operations" or "joined hand" operations.

The problem with these translations is that the resulting English terms are descriptively challenged; their meaning is not immediately obvious, and therefore more confusing than illuminating to the general public. Later authors, including S.A. Olson[57] and others, began to propose "sensing hands" or "touching hands" or "connecting hands" as more descriptive extrapolations of tuishou.

---

[55] Wen-Shan Huang, *"Fundamentals of Tai Chi Ch'uan"*, South Sky Book Company, Hong Kong,1973.

[56] Y.K.,Chen, *"Tai-Chi Ch'uan: Its Effects and Practical Applications,"* Newcastle Publishing Co. Inc., North Hollywood, CA,1979.

[57] Stuart Alve Olson, *"Tai Chi Sensing Hands,"* Unique Publications, 1999.

Why such resistance to the use of "pushing-hands?" Because, as a description of the activity it denotes, the terms tuishou or pushing hands are actually highly misleading. Here's why. Pushing hands literally communicates the idea of the hands engaged in pushing, and yet the worst thing to do in tuishou is to use strength and push with the hands to deliver force; doing so uses partial rather than integrated force, and will cause leaning and loss of balance if the opponent yields properly.

So actually, pushing-hands play should be called "no-pushing with hands" play. Indeed, the job of the hands is to sense, and not to generate or deliver the force. The division of labor for delivery we clearly established in previous chapters: the dantian generates the force at the center, and the legs, whose function it is to move the center and the body as a whole, actually deliver the force.

There can be no doubt that sensing hands, touching hands, connecting hands, and sticking hands are all preferable to pushing hands as more descriptive of the responsiveness training that is the essence of tuishou partnered activity. Yet to my way of thinking, these extrapolations all share a central deficiency in their expressed concern with the hands at the periphery of the body, whereas the essence of the game is to capture and gain control over the center of the opponent's body.

Since the object of the game and training is to control the opponent's central equilibrium through capturing her center, why not name the activity after the object of the game? The body part most prominently used, the hand, is only an extension of the central core. Hence my own candidate for a name that describes the purpose of the interactive training of tuishou, would be "capture the center." Yet, no matter how inadequate the term pushing-hands, it's usage persists and grows ever more widespread. All of us aspiring purists and reformers better recognize and accept that simple fact as well as its correlate that only in our teaching will we be able to transmit the deeper meaning through our touch.

···

The classics describe some of the essential skills developed in tuishou, first "listening and following" and then "yielding and sticking." Listening is a sensory skill while following is a motor skill; the level of their development and integration determines the skill-level of the player. Since we are talking about a tactile interchange, "listening" here means paying attention to stimuli with the skin as the organ of touch, and "following" means the ability to respond to this information, moving in any direction smoothly and without ever increasing the pressure at the point of contact.[58]

The skills of "listening" and "following" are defined by the ability to move in response to the opponent's movement without any change in pressure occurring at the point of contact. In a game where "timing is everything," if the listening and following skills are highly developed, the response will be simultaneous with the stimulus. When the listening and following skills are undeveloped or underdeveloped, the timing will be deficient and the result will be either increased resistance or structural collapse. Either will lead to loss of central equilibrium.

Yielding and sticking are two different ways to combine listening and following. Yielding refers to listening and following when the opponent is attacking and one is in the defensive mode; sticking refers to the listening and following one does on offense, while the opponent is trying to get away from us. Developmentally, the sensory skills of listening and following must first be learned by mastering the skill of yielding in the defensive mode. Then, on offense, they can be transferred and applied to learn sticking.

---

[58] It was pointed out to me in this connection that "just as we (in the west today) tend to privilege sight in our ways of speaking about reality ("I see what you mean," or "Let's illustrate that point by pointing out ..."), early Chinese thinkers tended to privilege hearing, likely because of the importance of following the commands of leaders. It is for that reason that ting 聽 "to hear, to listen" also means "to obey, to follow, to comply, to submit to, etc." So it already contains the meaning of responding and following. Louis Swaim, personal communication, 10/15/2011.

Master Tam's curriculum includes learning a great number of tuishou patterns and drills, drawn mostly from the various styles of taijiquan, yiquan, and xingyi. The best thing about learning many different patterns and then alternating and combining them in infinite variety is that the practice truly develops the sensory-motor integration necessary for the skills of listening and following.

The Responsiveness Skills: Listening and Following

From the point of view of the listening and following skills of responsiveness training, the dancing metaphor is very apt. In a partnered dance, where typically a man leads and a woman follows, the leading partner's hands and arms are unified with his torso into a frame that holds and guides the following partner. Depending on the skill level, that frame can vary. It may range from rigid, heavy strength to light, smooth elasticity, and the couple's movement will correspondingly vary from mechanical and awkward to smooth and fluid. Where skill is high, the leading partner indicates with the most subtle of touches and pressures where and how he wants his partner to move.

The following partner's skill is also necessary to the success of a partnered dance. If the following partner starts to have any ideas of her own about how she is going to move, she will step on the leading partner's toes or trip him, thereby destroying their timing. But if she lets herself be guided by her perceptual knowledge of the meaning of the leading partner's signals coupled with appropriate motor responsiveness, then the partners' combined skills can lead them to a high-level performance.

The quality of listening and following in dance is directly applicable to the tuishou encounter and can be utilized to reshape attitude and behavior. The key is to cultivate a state of readiness and willingness to respond by "dancing with" one's opponent and following the lead. One follows the opponent wherever she wants to go–all for the purpose of better controling her. Master Yang Chengfu was very clear on the dangers of taking the initiative and the advantages of limiting oneself to responsive action:

"Acting from yourself gets you stuck. Following the opponent keeps you free to move. If you can follow the opponent, you will obtain the subtlety of getting his attacks to land on nothing. If you try to act from yourself, you will not even be able to act from yourself. You can only act from yourself in the context of following the opponent."[59]

One trains one's self in listening and following by making a habit of paying very close attention to the two most significant variables in tuishou: (1) the distance between oneself and the opponent and (2) the pressure of the touch at the point of contact. Specifically, one should practice maintaining the pressure and distance at a constant level, adjusting the body through movement whenever the opponent tries to make a change. Personally, by maintaining this awareness, I'm constantly working to increase my responsiveness, learning valuable lessons and gaining helpful insights.

Controlling these variables of distance and pressure is essential in the contest for control of the opponent's center. If an opponent is coming towards me and I experience an increase either in pressure and/or the closing of the distance, I know that my timing and yielding response were deficient. Of course, the reverse is true as well. If the pressure increases when I move towards an opponent, I also know that her yielding is insufficient.

Why? Increased pressure indicates the receiving frame is too rigid and lacks adaptive elasticity; those faults allow an opponent to land. In other words, one who offers resistance invites an opponent to capture her center and asks to be bounced. But if an opponent is moving towards me and I experience the opposite, namely a decrease in pressure and/or an increase in the distance between us, then I know my response was anticipatory and I am running away. Conversely, if the pressure becomes lighter when she retreats, I know I'm not sticking to her properly, which will make capturing her center more difficult.

---

[59] Yang Chengfu, the Brennan translation, op.cit.

The internal martial artist seeks the same responsiveness skills (listening and following) as the dancing partner who follows, but for wholly different, if not opposite reasons. In dance, a responsive partner accepts the division of labor between leading and following in order to achieve a higher unity of coupled movement. For the internal martial artist, the quest for responsiveness in listening and following provides the means to assume control over the situation.

The Capturing Skill of Yielding

While tuishou shares the responsiveness skills of listening and following with ballroom dancing, pair figure-skating and other sports, there are two additional skills, yielding and sticking, that are essential for the internal martial arts. Yielding and sticking utilize the listening and following skills to capture the opponent's center of gravity and control her balance. Listening and following are responsiveness skills per se, whereas yielding and sticking are the capturing-the-center skills.

The purpose of yielding is to turn the tables on the attacker; yielding permits one to get in a better position to attack, that is, to connect and capture the opponent's center. The yielding strategy, then, is to go along with the opponent's initiative without resistance, but to "dance" just long enough to hijack the opponent's center and take over the lead without disclosing that intent.

From the perspective of the attacker who ends up captured because another has yielded properly, the experience is also best described by extending the dance analogy. It's as if you asked someone to dance, and she accepts and you begin dancing, effortlessly leading your partner. But all of a sudden the realization dawns on you that although you're still moving together effortlessly, things are no longer the same. While it's not evident to someone looking from the outside, everything has changed. You're no longer the one leading, but you are now the one following; your partner has subtly hijacked your control over the situation without your being aware of it and you're powerless to change anything.

Speaking personally again, I set myself the goal of becoming a good "dancer" and in so doing, cultivating my sensitivity and responsiveness. I wanted to be so responsive that an opponent could never lay a hand on me solidly enough to exert force. As my listening and following skills improved through such discipline, I found that my timing started to improve. Not thinking about attacking, I gained a lot of time to listen and to respond to my opponent's movements. Increasingly, I found myself able to respond to her attack well enough to draw her off balance and capture her center.

The skill of yielding utilizes the six-direction training we explored in Chapter 2 to capture the opponent's center. The six-direction training enables the yi to capture the opponent's center by instantly adjusting the tensile/elastic parameters of the body frame. That is, the defender's yi is able to modulate the frame, increasing or decreasing at will the internal pressure of the zhengti (coherent body or body frame) in precise response to the opponent's attack.

Although yielding can be done either with external movement or with internal movement, it is most often done through a combination of external movement and the inner modulation of the frame. In yielding with internal modulation of the frame, no external movement is visible. The opponent's energy is simply taken in at the point of contact and redistributed throughout the elastic tensegrity structure of the body frame to affect the capture of her center.

The lighter you can maintain the pressure at the point of contact, the easier it will be to yield and redirect the opponent's energy when attacked. Moreover, this principle of lightness of touch in yielding is expressed in Master Tam's summation, "You give your opponent the point of contact, but you do not give him the point of application of force." Also, use of the soft approach to get in underneath the opponent's perceptual radar will cause the involuntary tensing in her that allows connecting with and capturing her center, and controlling her balance. Indeed, for the internal martial artist, the "art" part is how to use the least amount of force in taking over and maintaining control of the opponent's center.

To capture your opponent in yielding (or sticking), subtly adjust any one of the four main variables in tuishou play, namely distance, speed, pressure and angle. When this is done below the threshold of perception, it will elicit a tension reaction, usually first the startle and then the opposition reflex, resulting in the opponent pushing herself off balance against your frame.

The Capturing Skill of Sticking

If yielding is the term we use to describe listening and following without force while being engaged defensively, sticking is the term we use for listening and following without force when we are engaged offensively. Yang Chengfu emphasized the interpenetrating, yin-yang nature of yielding and sticking when he wrote "... In sticking there is yielding and in yielding there is sticking. The active (yang) does not depart from the passive (yin) and the passive (yin) does not depart from the active (yang)..."[60] In other words, there is offense in defense and there is defense in offense. The former allows the instantaneous transformation of defense into offense when the opportunity presents itself, while the latter allows the instantaneous transformation of offense into defense when called for.

Yet, for all their mutual interpenetration, the yielding and sticking skills must be acquired sequentially. Only when the responsive skills of listening and following have been honed and perfected in yielding, the defensive capturing skill, can they then be applied to sticking, the offensive capturing skill. Like yielding, sticking exemplifies the skill of the "soft way of exerting force." In this context, visualize your touch as a piece of scotch tape. I used this term previously when describing Master Tam's touch. But to amplify the concept, imagine that no matter how your opponent tries to get away and shake it off, she cannot because your touch adheres.

And just as yielding is the defensive approach for controlling the opponent's center by causing her righting reflex to fail her so that she loses balance, so sticking is the offensive way of capturing the opponent's center by taking away her righting reflex. The soft-hands of the sticking power prevents the righting reflex of the opponent from functioning automatically by taking away the space the righting reflex needs for making the minute, unconscious and automatic adjustments to maintain balance.

---

[60] Yang Chengfu, the Brennan translation, op.cit.

This causes the opponent to freeze and leaves her unable to move. Because the sticking power works on the subtle level below the opponent's threshold of awareness, her reaction to the invasion of personal space is a subconscious whole-body tensing in a type of a startle reflex. The attacker only needs to maintain a soft frame; the defender will actually push herself off and away from that soft frame.

The importance of soft, relaxed hands cannot be overemphasized. The hands must be used as sensors, not battering rams. If the hands are hard with intention (to push and penetrate), they will have no sticking power. If the hands have force and momentum, they can be yielded to. If the hands flow like water, so soft that the opponent does not know they have entered her space, then all one has to do is connect them with the center and move forward. The opponent, having lost control of her center, will bounce away.

Sticking, like yielding, is a capturing skill, but it is used, not when the opponent is attacking, but when she is trying to yield to our attack. Thus it is not a skill of delivering the jin, but like yielding, it is a skill that creates the moment for delivering the jin. If my sticking ability is better than my opponent's yielding ability, then I will be able to cut off the angle of her retreat, causing her to stiffen involuntary, and I'll be able to bounce her.

Obstacles to Responsiveness

Assuming a willing and able teacher, a student's mastery of internal martial arts responsiveness is largely dependent on overcoming certain fundamental psychological and biological obstacles. Psychologically, the positive role of belief in successful endeavors is well-known and documented. The more we believe in the overall truth and practical feasibility of the project and our own capacity to fulfill our part in it, the more successful the endeavor will be.

The "overall truth" part is easy. Of course when people first hear about Master Tam's abilities, many flat-out refuse to believe that such things are possible. But once they have been in Master Tam's presence these doubts evaporate like fog in the warming sun. His skills are demonstrable, and the results are undisputedly repeatable and predictable to everyone's satisfaction—even if many are baffled by what they see.

The second part, coming to believe we're capable of doing it ourselves, is infinitely more difficult. Students need to grow into the belief and realization that Master Tam's skills can be learned. Self doubt is often aggravated by a lack of clarity. We are in the dark about how Master Tam does what he does so effectively, because the main event occurs below the threshold of our perception. Because we cannot (yet) feel what is going on, it is difficult to think about it with any conceptual clarity.

A further problem is that any self-doubt in this respect is likely to have negative effects. Usually, it leads to a slackening of the effort and discipline necessary to achieve sure and subtle responsiveness; in many cases, doubt will cause the student to adopt substitute methods and strategies that hide the lack of true achievement. My own story, as I will detail later, was a case of the latter. To mask my lack of progress in the responsiveness and capturing skills (listening and following, yielding and sticking), I developed some facility and quickness of hands that allowed me to exploit the openings and gaps in the defenses of my opponent. By opting for the easier, short-term gain of winning, rather than sticking to the principle, I lost my way.

...

But perhaps the greatest obstacles to mastery of voluntary modulation of the elastic frame are the involuntary reactions at opposite ends of the "reaction to threat" spectrum. These are the hardwired yin-yang of the opposition-resistance and collapsing-withdrawal reflexes, respectively, that we share with many animals. To summarize our previous discussion in Chapter 3, the opposition reflex causes us to push back when a force is applied against us, and the accomodation reflex causes us to withdraw when resistance is judged futile.

The relevance of this to the practice of tuishou and the internal martial arts is profound. As explored repeatedly in these chapters, whenever an opponent applies force to our body, we involuntarily stiffen our frame to resist and push back—this is the the opposition reflex at work. Likewise, whenever an opponent applies force to our body and we experience the involuntary collapse of our frame, the accommodation reflex is at work.

Defensively, the fundamental object of tuishou training is to replace the involuntary opposition/resistance and withdrawal/collapse reflexes with the voluntary yielding response. Those who are too hard to begin with must become softer and those who are too soft to begin with must firm up, all in the search of that happy medium of elasticity of frame and correct timing that allows control over the opponent. In this respect I've observed a general correlation/association with gender. As I've mentioned previously, in my experience men tend toward opposition reflex, while women tend toward the collapsing reflex. In the internal martial arts, neither is constructive.

The learning and unlearning process takes time. Often, while striving to become soft and not engage in the opposition reflex, the tuishou practitioner goes to the other extreme and collapses her structure. Or, if her initial tensency is to collapse her frame, in trying to give it more substance she will often overdo it and make it too rigid. Indeed, gaining mastery over the skill of yielding sometimes seems like a never–ending string of involuntary tensions (stiffenings) and relaxations (collapses). Slowly, little by little, a student learns to modulate her frame voluntarily between these two involuntarily extremes, as she learns to respond and yield in real time.

Bear in mind that the strategy of responsiveness works in two directions. The same involuntary reflexes that we seek to replace with voluntary responses in ourselves, we seek to induce in our opponents, so we can take advantage of them. The sensitivity we develop leads to the ability to induce the opposition and collapsing reflexes at a very subtle level in our opponents. By inducing these reflexes, we become able to connect with and capture the central equilibrium of our opponents. Also bear in mind that in tuishou play, my opponent is trying to do the very same thing I'm trying to do, namely prevent her own involuntary reflexes of resistance and collapse and induce them in me. In that sense, tuishou is a competition for control played out between two persons on the subtlest levels of sensory motor interaction.

Part 4

On Shen

Transcending Power through
Enlightened Awareness

Chapter 9: The Neurology of the Spirit and the Varieties of Transcendent Experience

Shen: The Spirit of Awareness

In Chinese culture, shen, usually translated as spirit or spirit of awareness, is understood as operating in at least three different realms. On a cosmic scale, shen refers to the élan vital of the universe. On a human level, it refers to the vitality of an individual. Thirdly, shen refers to the wondrous skills and acts performed under the influence of cosmic inspiration, as in true artistic mastery and creativity.[61]

Perhaps the prototypical example of the shen state of enlightenment in Chinese literature is the hero of one of Zhuangzi's most famous tales, Pao Ding, whom I mention in the introduction to this volume. Pao Ding was a servant of a great lord by the name of Wenhui, and his job was jack of all trades around the kitchen – butcher, cook and clean-up boy all wrapped up in one

Fig. 39
Pao Ding

(Fig. 39). Word got around the palace and the village that Pao Ding was someone special; that to behold him cutting up an ox and preparing it for his lord's consumption was a wondrous spectacle, a veritable dance in which the distinctions between knife and man and ox disappeared. People marveled and his fame spread. Indeed, so great was Pao Ding's skill in the art of dismemberment that for almost twenty years, he not only never had to replace his knife, but he never even had to sharpen it. Of course, the Lord Wenhui was probably the last to hear about Pao Ding's amazing skills, but when he did he summoned his servant for a public show and tell.

The lowly kitchen servant turned out to be quite the sage and he had a thing or two to share with his worldly lord, who had so much wealth and power in the material realm, about the spiritual realm of shen and enlightenment.

---

[61] Kuang-Ming Wu, "*The Butterfly as Companion: Meditations on the First Three Chapters of the Chuang Tzu,*" State University of New York Press, New York,1990, pp. 319-20.

Fortunately, Pao Ding did not disappoint his lord; his performance was sublime, sending the lord into ecstatic admiration for Pao Ding's embodiment of the Dao and his mastery of wuwei, the doing by not doing, the way of least resistance. As Zhuangzi tells the story: Pao Ding loses himself in his attentiveness and lets his knife find its own easy way into the crevasses and interstices of the carcass. His lord, watching, exults that in this dance with the ox, life and death are joined in a Dance of Life. Lord Wenhui realizes that he is witnessing in this dance a celebration of the death of the ox as a way of providing nourishment for the living: incrementally, as if in slow motion and of its own accord, the animal falls apart into pieces, ready for further preparation and cooking.

After the event, genuinely curious but as ever inclined towards the practical, Lord Wenhui asks his servant to describe how he does what he does and how he learned to do it. As to the first question Pao Ding relates that "my skill is beyond skill; it is the dao." After decades of cutting up oxen he knows their anatomy so well that he can feel "the space that is always there where part meets part." And handling his knife during all that time he has learned to feel the "thicklessness" of the knife at its very edge. Thus, Pao Ding explains to his lord, what he does is simply "insert an instrument that has no thickness into a structure that is amply spaced, and it surely cannot fail to have plenty of room."[62]

As to the second question, Pao Ding sums up in a few simple sentences the stages that marked his progression toward effortless mastery. In the initial, apprentice-like stage, he was awed by the enormity of the task at hand, and so preoccupied with the ox that it became a near obsession, "When I began cutting up oxen, all I could see was the ox itself."[63] Lacking skill and not knowing the ox and its parts, he could only resort to brute force (li) to accomplish his goal, and undoubtedly ruined a few good knives in the process. As he progressed into the middle stage in his developmment, the tension dissipated; relaxation and centering came, bringing with it changes in sensory motor integration that gave him a more focused perception of detail and fine muscular control. "After three years, I no longer saw the whole ox."[64]

---

[62] Ibid, p. 286.
[63] Ibid, p. 317.
[64] Ibid.

He had come to see only the specific places where his intent guided both eye and hand. In this yi stage, his sharply focused intent controlled his movements and his tools ever more precisely and efficiently. "And now--now I go at it by spirit and don't look with my eyes. Perception and understanding have come to a stop and…the spirit meets the ox, in which it walks as it desires."[65] In this final stage of ultimate mastery, shen, the flow of spiritual vitality pervades his knife as it dances with the ox. In this stage, all sensory and cognitive faculties recede; Pao Ding, the knife and the ox, all three become one in the effortlessness movement of the spirit.

The concept of shen as non-substantial, enlightened spirit that effortlessly produces substantial results is closely akin to the Daoist art of "wuwei." Wuwei is often interpreted as "achieving everything by doing nothing." Actually it would be more accurate to say that it consists of not doing anything more than absolutely necessary. Pao Ding hardly moves, and yet the ox "loosens" and falls apart. The way of wuwei is the path of knowing things intimately, thereby following them as they unfold in their natural course of development, and nudging them along at critical junctures to obtain the desired results.

In "The Butterfly as Companion," Professor Kuang-Ming Wu remarks that "…the resemblance of [Pao Ding's] movement to that of taijiquan… is uncanny. Taijiquan is a lethal art and an art of life; so is butchery."[66] Professor Wu's description of the dynamics of the Pao Ding's art is almost identical with his descriptions of the internal martial arts: "…the Life energy (qi, if you will) flows freely from the center of the bodily gravity (tan tien) through the meridian artery, and the flow is manifested in the butcher's knife as it stays on route."[67]

Like butchery, the internal martial arts are arts of dismemberment. Of course, the first dismembers dead carcasses, whereas the latter "dismembers" living human beings. Reading Professor Kuang's analysis and commentary on the shen stage of Pao Ding, I found myself musing (not to take anything away from Pao Ding's achievement) that it is still an order of magnitude more difficult to artfully disarm, or dismember, either figuratively or literally, a living human opponent than an already dead animal. Realizing this has deepened my appreciation of Master Tam, who is a true, living embodiment of the shen or spirit stage that Zhuangzi so succinctly describes in the ancient tale of Pao Ding.

---

[65] Ibid, p. 339-40.
[66] Ibid.
[67] Ibid, p. 339.

However significant the distinctions between the two, martial arts mastery goes through the same stages and adheres to the same principles as Pao Ding's art. The internal martial arts subscribe to and partake in the wuwei way of life, and like Pao Ding, the internal martial artist works toward the state of shen. Both achieve their goal without use of force, their augmented awareness enabling them to avoid resistance and exert the minimum of physical effort necessary.

Moreover, both share in a double enlightenment of ends and means. Both use the tactile sense as the means of experiencing shen. Pao Ding senses and is aware of the spaces between the structures and is able to insert there the nothing at the edge of the blade and to separate the structure effortlessly. Likewise, Master Tam senses and is more aware of the deficiencies and excesses in an opponent's equilibrium and frame than the opponent himself. Working below his opponent's radar, Master Tam is able to capture and control the opponent's central equilibrium—and the opponent never realizes it until it is too late. Without use of force, Master Tam can bounce an opponent many feet away, drop him to the floor, or incapacitate him in a myriad of other ways.

What goes on in the brain of the superb artists such as Pao Ding or Master Tam when they experience shen, this sublime spirit of awareness, while engaged in the exercise of their skill? In Part 3 we saw that the yi, or intention, is the mental faculty associated with the frontal lobe. This chapter focuses on the shen, or spirit, as the mental faculty associated with the parietal lobe. We begin by exploring the neurological basis of peak or transcendent experiences.

The Nervous System, the Rhythm of Daily Life and Peak Experiences

Deep in the brain sits the hypothalamus (see Fig. 31), the master gland that controls the autonomic, or involuntary, nervous system. Secretions by the hypothalamic core activate the parasympathetic nervous system, while secretions by the hypothalamic cortex stimulate the sympathetic nervous system. Between them they govern the fundamental biological cycle of energy expenditure and replenishment.

The parasympathetic system, often referred to as the quiescent system, operates when the organism is in relative harmony with its environment, not moving much or at all, eating and digesting, resting and sleeping, etc. As the restoration of depleted energy reserves can take place most efficiently when body and mind are in a state of maximum relaxation, the motor (musculature) system is dialed down to a minimum when the parasympathetic system is operating. The effect of para-sympathetic stimulation on the perceptual system is to induce a relaxed state of soft focus where perception widens as attention softens. Soft focus causes a blurring of boundaries between objects, and the distinctions between foreground and background disappear into a single awareness of the whole perceptual field.

The effect of the sympathetic stimulation on both muscular and perceptual systems is the exact opposite. Often referred to as the arousal or crisis system, the sympathetic nervous system initiates and sustains all effort made by the perceptual and motor systems involved in the expenditure of any physical and mental energy. Sympathetic nervous stimulation marshals the body's musculature for use as it focuses attention narrowly on the object of perception, sharply demarcating the boundaries between the foreground and background, between self and the object of attention, reshaping the environment in our favor and according to our wishes.

In everyday life, we, our conscious egos, live and dwell in the brain's frontal lobes where our yi plans and decides our voluntary acts and utterances. Of course any decision or plan can only be as good as the information it is based on. And all such planning and decision-making by the yi in the frontal lobes is based on the perceptual content of the parietal lobes, which are the sensory hubs that integrate the awareness of the space surrounding us and our body's position within it. For that reason, in ordinary circumstances the parietal lobe plays a subordinate and supporting role to the frontal lobe.

The parietal lobes integrate our body schema, our sense of balance and physical wholeness into one awareness. An incredible amount of highly-processed information from all major senses, including touch, proprioception, vision, hearing, and balance, are integrated in the parietal lobes to create the sense of our embodied self embedded in a wider world. This is far more information than the yi needs and wants for its focusing and decision-making processes. And so the yi acts as a de facto filter to exclude all parietal information that is not immediately relevant to the intention developed by the yi. Most generally, of course, the yi directs the motor system to achieve specific tasks of movement or speech.

...

While the rhythms of ordinary, daily life are regulated largely by the alternating activity of the sympathetic and parasympathetic nervous systems, periodically our ordinary, daily life is punctuated by experiences so intense that, in sharp contrast to the humdrum cycles of daily life, they stand out as extra-ordinary, and are therefore often called 'peak' or 'transcendent' experiences (the terms are used interchangeably here). Individuals often remember such experiences as highly significant and meaningful for the future, either to be sought after because of their positive intensity, or to be avoided because of their negative intensity.

Transcendent experiences come in great variety. Perhaps amongst the most common are those evolved by nature to assure the continuation of the species, in particular orgasm and childbirth. Often people who come close to dying as a result of an accident report transcendent perceptual experiences. Likewise, war and athletics frequently generate transcendent experiences in participants. The practice of arts and crafts also can generate transcendent experiences. Finally religious and spiritual practices of all kinds are also well known to induce transcendent experience.

An important consequence of the inter-related roles played by the frontal lobes as motor centers and the parietal lobes as a sensory centers is that it defines their relationship to time. Ordinarily, the frontal lobe's intentional function is oriented towards the future, while the parietal lobe's orientational function maps the self within its contemporaneous spatial environment. In other words, the parietal lobe integrates the current perceptions of the separate senses into a holistic representation of our body in external space in the present moment of time.

Under normal circumstances, then, this information about the present moment is routed to the frontal lobe to be used by the yi as the basis for planning and executing plans and activities in the future, anywhere from immediate to distant. Such planning and decision-making functions of the yi, furthermore, are always based, either implicitly or explicitly, on the memories of the past, stored in yet other areas of the brain.

What gives rise to the experience of shen, the spirit of awareness, is a reversal of roles between frontal and parietal lobe functions as the dominant and subordinate partners. Under ordinary circumstances, the frontal lobes are dominant and the parietal lobes are subordinate. In transcendent experience, however, frontal lobe functions are de-activated while parietal lobe functions are hyper-activated. This de-activation of the frontal lobes also explains why during transcendent experience, awareness of both future and past are absent; in the intensity of peak experience there is no past or future time, but only the present moment as constituted by parietal lobes.

The two brain regions that play major roles in the production of transcendent experience are the orientation association areas (OAA, see fig. 30) of both left and right parietal lobes. The function of the left orientation association area is to map the boundaries of our physical self. The function of the right orientation association area is to map the surrounding physical space and to place the body within the context of the three-dimensional environment. What happens in each area under simultaneous stimulation by both the parasympathetic and sympathetic nervous system is what determines the form and content of transcendent experiences.

In the sections that follow, we will explore the most fundamental categories of peak experiences and their defining characteristics. This survey will provide us with a basis for understanding the essential nature of the shen of the internal martial artist. We will begin by considering why the sensory-motor dynamics of sexual orgasm makes it the prototype for all peak experiences. Next, we will meet the mystics of the body, a large group, consisting of athletes and artists and the like, whose peak experiences result from sensory-motor engagement with the world. Finally, we will encounter another very large group, whom I call the athletes of the mind because they pursue peak experiences through intentional sensory-motor disengagement from the world.

Sex: Primordial Prototype of Transcendent Experience

The ecstasies of sex are primarily the result of two interconnected positive feedback loops. One is between the sensory and motor systems and the other is between the sympathetic and parasympathetic nervous systems. The initial phase of the sexual act consists of increasing parasympathetic stimulation of the body and mind primarily through tactile interaction. Experientially, the tactile sensations generate the feeling of a pleasurable expansion of the physical body. The intensification of tactile sensual pleasure leads to the secondary phase that is initiated and sustained by the sympathetic nervous system and characterized by an increasing motor response by the muscular system. The increase of sensation intensifies muscular activity, and vice versa, the increase in muscular activity intensifies the pleasurable sensations. Thus, in a very special feedback loop, sex combines the ecstasy of harmony with the urgency of emergency.

Moreover, as the sympathetic stimulation drives the increased exertions of the motor system, the general tactile well-being generated by the parasympathetic system becomes increasingly focused on and intensified in the genitals. Focused thus, this dynamic creates a kind of urgency in which the pressure of pleasure becomes so great as to become unbearable. As the pressure of pleasure builds, the body becomes ever more insistent on reaching the climax of explosive release. Eventually, inexorably, the interaction culminates in the orgasmic discharge of the built up energy through the mechanism of the whole body reflex.

The intensity of the orgasm experience derives from this simultaneous maximum activation of both the sympathetic and parasympathetic nervous systems. As Newberg put it, "...orgasm requires the simultaneous stimulation of both the arousal and quiescent systems."[68] In this it is prototypical, for the intensity of all other peak or transcendent experiences is characterized first and foremost by the simultaneous activation of both parasympathetic and sympathetic systems. Again, in Newberg's words, "the very neurological structures and pathways involved in transcendent experiences–including the arousal, quiescent and limbic systems–evolved primarily to link sexual climax to the powerful sensation of orgasm."[69]

---

[68] Andrew Newberg, M.D. and Eugene d'Aquili, M.D., Ph.D., "*Why God Won't Go Away: Brain Science & the Biology of Belief*", Ballantine Books, New York, 2001, p.125.

[69] Ibid.

Next, we must come to a better understanding of the second feature that is characteristic of all transcendent experiences, namely, the neural mechanism that produces the experience of merger or union. Here again the salient facts of what occurs during sexual arousal and orgasm provides a template for understanding what occurs in other types of peak experiences. Most basic here is the functional change in the relationship between the frontal and parietal lobes during the sexual experience. This change consists of the inhibition of the frontal lobe yi functions and an augmentation of the function of the parietal lobes. Normally the intensity of the present moment in the sexual experience requires the yi and the frontal lobe to dial down and stop operation. It is a sure bet that if intellectual and analytical functions continue to dominate, the experience will be diminished.

The parietal lobe, on the other hand, is more active than ever during the sexual act, its function being to integrate the perceptual data of the present moment, and to map the physical body relative to the three-dimensional space surrounding it. Due to the high level of parasympathetic stimulation, the left parietal orientation area, in charge of mapping the body's boundaries, begins to experience and map those boundaries as less distinct and sharp and more expansive and diffuse. In the right parietal orientation area, the increasing intensity of the tactile stimulation crowds out the normally important visual component in mapping the body's position in three dimensional space, and leaves the tactile stimulation as the sole input. Combined, the left and right parietal association areas produce the totality of the sensation of the physical boundaries (skin) expanding and merging with one's partner. This is the neurological basis for the feeling of lovers that they are mutually dissolving in an ocean of reciprocal tactile bliss.

In conclusion, what the orgasm as prototype of all transcendent experience tells us is that all peak or transcendent experiences are characterized by the following three things:

- simultaneous and maximum activation of the sympathetic and parasympathetic nervous systems;
- the inhibition of frontal lobe functions and augmentation of the parietal lobe functions; and

- the experience of merger or union, consisting of the blurring of the body's physical boundaries, as perceived in the left parietal orientation area, and the subsequent experience of merger of the self with the sensory content of the right parietal orientation area.

In addition, we will discover that the great variety of peak experiences, and differences in them, are determined by the order of activation of parasympathetic and sympathetic systems and by the specific sensory content of the right parietal orientation area.

Mystics of the Body: Transcendence through Sensory-Motor Engagement with the World

I use the term "mystics of the body" to denote those individuals who have transcendent experiences as a result of their perceptual and motor engagement with the world around them (Fig. 40). The focus of this engagement may be war, sports, arts, crafts or other endeavors. A defining difference between the transcendent experience of orgasm and the shen experience by the mystics of the body lies in the nature of the sensory input that is the source of the experience. The senses most deeply involved in bringing on the ecstatic experience of sexual orgasm are the proximity senses of touch, taste and smell; the distance senses of vision and hearing, though they may be important in the onset, fade to secondary importance as the interaction progresses. For the mystics of the body, however, while the proximity senses may be involved, usually the distance senses of vision and hearing, and in particular vision, trigger the experience of augmented awareness, or shen.

Fig. 40
Mystics of the Body

Combat euphoria is perhaps the clearest and most fundamental example of the transcendent experience of those whom we can identify as mystics of the body. Under the intense demands of a drawn-out battle, combat euphoria occurs when warriors push their bodies beyond normal limits and tap the absolute last reserves of physical and mental power to stave off death and remain alive. At such moments, the doors to infinite realms of perception and power can suddenly open and result in a transcendent experience. Athletes, especially at the highest level of sport, have near identical peak experiences. For one, practically all sports, whether solitary or team efforts, have their roots in the hunting and warring activities of our primitive forebears. Competitions in running, fighting, swimming, jumping, throwing spears and stones, shooting arrows—all these were tests of an individual's abilities as a hunter and warrior. Likewise the equipment used in modern sports, such as balls and bats, sticks and rackets, javelins and epees, derive from the weapons that were implements of survival in more distant times. As the basketball great Bill Russell once remarked, all sports are "a mixture of art and war."[70]

The neurological progression and the dynamic between the sensory and motor component that produces the transcendent experience of the mystics of the body is the reverse of what happens in the sexual peak experience. In sex the initial activation starts with the parasympathetic stimulation through the tactile sensory system, which induces the secondary activation of the sympathetic nervous system and ever intensifying motor activity and effort. With the mystics of the body, the initial phase of the experience consists of continuous motor activity and sympathetic nervous system stimulation. Sustained to the point of depletion and exhaustion, this dynamic eventually triggers the secondary phase, activation of the parasympathetic nervous system, which by masking the feelings of exhaustion and depletion through feelings of invulnerability and euphoria, enables a last surge of energy and effort.

In the peak experience of the mystics of the body we find the same features that characterize the peak experience of sex: the de-activation of the frontal lobe and the yi, the augmentation of parietal lobe functions, and the corresponding alterations in the perceptions of space and time. Michael Murphy, in his fascinating book, *"In the Zone: Transcendent Experience in Sports,"*[71] quotes numerous famous athletes who describe a sense of space as augmented and expanded, and an awareness of time without past or future but only an endless present.

The football great John Brody said "… time seems to slow way down, in an uncanny way, as if everyone were moving in slow motion. It seems as if I had all the time in the world to watch the receivers run their patterns. I know the defensive line is coming at me just as fast as ever. And yet the whole thing seems like a movie or a dance in slow motion."[72]

---

[70] Andrew Cooper, *"Playing in the Zone: Exploring the Spiritual Dimensions of Sports,"* Shambhala, Boston & New York, 1998, p.129.

[71] Michael,Murphy, *"In the Zone: Transcendent Experience in Sports,"* Penguin, New York, NY,1995, p. 38.

[72] Ibid, p. 42.

Basketball's legendary Bill Russell also noted: "At that special level ... it's almost as if we were playing in slow motion. I could almost sense how the next play would develop and where the next shot would be taken ... My premonitions would be consistently correct."[73] Here again, in the immediacy of the present moment—a moment of life or death in war, win or lose in an athletic contest—there is simply no time for the yi and its past or future concerns. Along with the yi, in the face of the overwhelming needs of the present moment, the ego (and its language functions) are inhibited, and the loss of these functions is as characteristic of the transcendent experience for mystics of the body as for the experience of sexual union.

Space, on the other hand, is perceived by these mystics of the body in times of sustained crisis as greatly expanded to include the totality of one's surrounding space and position within it. Bobby Orr, the Hall of Fame hockey great was famous for being able to see all the action on the ice and knowing where everyone was going to be moments before they got there.[74] Likewise, the soccer superstar Pele: "... at any instant ... seemed to know the position of all the players on the field, and to sense what each man was going to do next."[75] Bob Cousy of basketball renown also agreed: "I can see more than most people out of the corners of my eyes. I don't have to turn my head to find out what's going on at either side. It sometimes appears that I'm throwing the ball without looking. I'm looking all right, but out of the corner of my eyes."[76]

For a mystic of the body—an athlete, a warrior, an artist, a craftsman—it is this heightened awareness of the body in surrounding space and a precise, almost effortless ability to control the body even in the most challenging circumstances that characterizes the experience of shen. The peak experience of the mystics of the body confirms that the neurological mechanism involved in shen is the result of the inhibition of the focusing and intentional functions of the frontal lobe yi, upon which the entire content of the parietal lobes fills the field of perceptual awareness. For the mystics of the body, this content is primarily visual, particularly the holistic function of mapping the body within the context of surrounding space.

---

[73] Ibid, p. 50.

[74] Ibid, p. 38.

[75] Ibid, p. 50.

[76] Ibid, p. 39.

Recall that the mapping of our surrounding personal space is a function of the right parietal orientation area and the mapping of the body's boundaries within it is a function of the left orientation area. For the mystics of the body, therefore, shen is an experience of the intimate unity of the self with the external environment. Distinctions made in "ordinary reality" between foreground and background, subject and object, are no longer applicable because there is only the experiential unity, or union, of the bodily self sensing and moving within the environment.

Athletes of the Mind: Transcendence through Sensory-Motor Disengagement from the World

We have seen that the peak experiences of the mystics of the body are generated by crisis that occurs during times of full engagement with the external world. By their very nature, peak experiences of this kind are unpredictable. You never know when they are going to happen. Additionally, there is always the possibility of something going wrong causing the euphoric high from successful use of motor activity in the face of crisis to flip into its opposite—motor paralysis, panic and terror.

As a consequence, throughout the ages people who sought transcendent experiences have looked for ways to reduce the possibility of unintended negative outcomes. By following the exact opposite strategy, namely the path of dis-engagement and non-interaction with the world, some have discovered more predictable and less dangerous ways to ensure positive transcendent experiences. I refer here to the meditators, monks, priests, nuns and lay practitioners of all religious and spiritual traditions worldwide who habitually withdraw from ordinary, daily life, to a safe, quiet place to meditate or pray in quest of mystical union and merger.

In order to produce peak experiences, sensory-motor disengagement needs be prolonged. Any such effort can be sustained only by the continuous application of intention and the will. As Newberg et al wrote, "Transcendent mystical experiences...depend on the involvement of higher cognitive structures, especially those found in the frontal lobe and other association areas."[77] The use of mental effort by the yi to create the proper conditions for inducing transcendent experience is universal to all religious and spiritual traditions. I refer collectively to the practitioners of this methodology as "athletes of the mind" (Fig. 41) because their mental effort in maintaining

Fig. 41
Athletes of the Mind

---

[77] Andrew Newberg, M.D. and Eugene d'Aquili, M.D., Ph.D., "*Why God Won'tGo Away: Brain Science & the Biology of Belief*", Ballantine Books, New York, 2001, p.125.

sensory-motor disengagement from the world often resembles that of the endurance athlete who extends his physical effort by sheer force of will.

As with the mystics of the body, the peak experiences of the athletes of the mind also consist of simultaneous activation of both branches of the autonomic system --the sympathetic and parasympathetic nervous systems--by the hypothalamus. However, for the athlete of the mind, the progression of events is the exact reverse of that experienced by the mystic of the body: the systemic parasympathetic stimulation is primary and the systemic sympathetic stimulation is secondary.

The achievement of the athletes of the mind is strangely paradoxical in that their yi creates a crisis that then results in the yi's de-activation. Let us untangle the thread by understanding the progression of events. The sequence begins with the interaction of the yi (attention association area or AAA), the hypothalamus and the parietal lobe to get the necessary circuits between them going in a positive feedback loop. When one closes the eyes and otherwise minimizes sensory stimulation while sitting quietly and/or engaging in simple, repetitive motor activity,[78] the yi affects the systemic parasympathetic stimulation by the hypothalamic core, which results in a general feeling of well-being, ease, calm and comfort.[79] The hypothalamus in turn sends impulses back to the frontal lobes' AAA, which sends them back again to the hypothalamus, fostering deeper and deeper levels of calm.

Following the laws of polarity in which conditions eventually turn into their opposites, the yi's maintenance of this sense of harmony over an extended period of time becomes itself a type of crisis. As contemplation deepens and the yi sustains the behavior beyond a certain point, the increasing stimulation of the hypothalamic core and the parasympathetic system builds until, at its peak, spillover occurs, causing the hypothalamic cortex to activate the sympathetic nervous system.[80] It is at this point of simultaneous activation of the parasympathetic and sympathetic nervous systems that the athletes of the mind experience shen. What is important here is to note that this is the mirror image of the process that occurs in the mystics of the body. For the mystics of the body, the cortex of the hypothalamus first activates the sympathetic system and secondarily, the hypothalamic core stimulates parasympathetic system.

---

[78] Like the orgastic peak experience, that of the athletes of the mind also utilizes sustained simple repetitive motor movement that drives the dynamic towards simultaneous activation of parasympathetic and sympathetic systems. From this perspective, the practice of sustained stillness amounts to a special case of sustained motor movement. The continous effort by the yi to maintain stillness and not move is as strenuous as the continuous effort by the yi to sustain repetitive movement.

[79] Herbert Benson, M.D., "*Timeless Healing: The Power of Biology and Belief,*" Fireside, New York, NY,1997.

[80] Eugene d'Aquili and Andrew Newberg, "*The Mystical Mind: Probing the Biology of Religious Experience,*" Fortress Press, Minneapolis, p. 112.

Monks, nuns and lay people of all stripes and colors, including ecstatic Sufi dancers, entranced orthodox Jews bowing to the Wailing Wall, the chanters of "om" and other mantras, the contemplators of sacred images or yantras, the practitioners of sexual rituals or tantras, the pursuers of the void or the plenum—all use the yi to sustain selective stimulation of the sensory-motor apparatus. Maintaining focus on one or more of the senses while engaging in repetitive motor activity for long periods of time, the athletes of the mind disengage from the world to pursue union with the divine.

As with the peak experiences of the mystics of the body, so with the athletes of the mind: the parietal lobes' orientation association areas provide the content of the transcendent experience. Recall that the normal everyday function of the left and right orientation association areas, respectively, is to define the boundaries of the self and to map the spatial matrix in which the self exists. The effects of the yi's sustained focus in deep prayer or meditation on both orientation association areas is profound. Neural activity in the left parietal orientation association is inhibited, which causes the perceived boundaries of the self to soften, while the right orientation association area has nothing to work with except whatever the yi (attention association area) is focused on. In other words, it is the yi and its focus that will determine the nature of the transcendent experience, whether it be union with non-being, union with a supreme being, or union with any other object of contemplation.

In case of the Zen monk, for example, the monk uses his yi to maintain sensory deprivation and motor deactivation. Deprived of input, the left orientation association area, becomes

Fig. 42
Union with the Void

incapable of finding the boundaries of the body, resulting in the mind's perception of the self becoming limitless as it stops perceiving any self at all. The right orientation association area, lacking the information it needs to create a spatial context in which the self can be oriented, instead generates a sense of absolute spacelessness, or spaciousness (Fig. 42). The combined deactivation of both left and right orientation association areas results in neurological reality consistent with the descriptions of ultimate spiritual union; no discrete objects, no sense of space or the passage of time, no demarcation between self and universe. In fact, there is no sense of subjective self at all, only an absolute sense of unity without thought, without words, and without sensation.[81]

81 Ibid, p. 119.

In the spiritual or religious traditions that use images, objects, or activities in devotional practices, the effect on the left orientation area is the same. It also becomes incapable of finding and defining the boundaries of the body. But the effect on the right orientation association area is correspondingly different. The attention association area (yi) stimulates the right parietal orientation area to focus more and more intensely on the object or image of contemplation, such as Christ, Buddha or Shiva, until all else is excluded. In such single-minded contemplation, the image utilized enlarges until it is perceived as constituting the whole depth and breadth of reality. Coupled with the deactivation of the left orientation association area, and the softening of the perceived boundaries of the self, the mind is led to the startling perception that the individual self has been mystically absorbed into the transcendent reality of Christ, Buddha or Shiva (Fig. 43).[82]

Fig. 43
Union with the
Object of Contemplation

The Shen of the Internal Martial Artist

We now come full circle to apply the insights gained to understanding the shen of the internal martial artist. For convenience of comparison, the main findings are summarized in Table 1 below and show the transcendent experience of the internal martial artist to be a kind of middle way between the mystic of the body and the athlete of the mind. With the the mystics of the body, internal martial artists share the full sensory-motor engagement with the world as the experiential basis of shen. With the athletes of the mind, internal martial artists share the approach to attaining the shen state, using the yi to achieve systemic parasympathetic stimulation and progressive relaxation.

Recall the salient points of how the method of relaxation produces the necessary integration of both the motor and sensory components to achieve shen. Internal martial artists use standing meditation as the fundamental relaxation technique to raise the level of functional integration of the machinery of posture and movement. Standing practice unifies the bones, muscles and connective tissue into a structure that has both great stability and strength and unparalleled agility and responsiveness.

[82] Andrew Newberg, M.D. and Eugene d'Aquili, M.D., Ph.D., "*Why God Won't Go Away: Brain Science & the Biology of Belief*", Ballantine Books, New York, 2001, p.122.

Slowly, as the muscles one-by-one become simultaneously more relaxed and more toned, they become more and more integrated; that integration increasingly come under voluntary control, first by the yi and then by the shen, and guides the motor apparatus in yielding, sticking and the issuance of fajin. These are the internal martial arts faps (fixed action patterns) that increase the probability of a positive experience of shen. Through training, these faps become so ingrained they can operate successfully without guidance of the frontal lobes, based solely on the holistic perception of the parietal lobes.

Table 1: Peak Experiences and their Characteristics

PEAK EXPERIENCE	Mystics of the Body (including external martial arts)	Athletes of the Mind	Internal Martial Arts
Primary Activation	Sympathetic Nervous System	Parasympathetic Nervous System	Parasympathetic Nervous System
Secondary Activation	Parasympathetic Nervous system	Sympathetic Nervous system	Sympathetic Nervous System
Sensory Perception	Engaged; Focussed externally on touch, sight & sound	Disengaged; Focussed internally on object of contemplation	Engaged; Focussed internally on kinesthetics & balance; Focussed externally on touch, sight & sound
Motor Behavior	Engaged & Responsive	Disengaged & Repetitive	Engaged & Responsive
Merger of Perceiver & Perceived	With External Reality: Self, Foreground & Background	With Internal Reality (provided by yi)	With External Reality: Self, Inner ground, Foreground & Background

In the sensory realm, the process of progressive relaxation and integration is much the same. At first, of necessity, the yi can only train one sense at the time. The training is therefore sequential. Initially, in our solo work of standing and moving meditation, we train the inner senses of balance, proprioception, and modulation of effort. Next, in our partnered exercises we train the proximity sense of touch and the distance senses of sight and sound. The training for each sense is the same, to expand the range of its perception through relaxation, opening up sight, sound, smell and touch to take in the world around us. It is learning to habitually be in a soft focus mode rather than a hard focus mode. Such relaxation training of each individual sense, while still directed by the frontal lobe's yi and thus still partial, is the first step towards accessing the parietal lobe's holistic shen, where all the senses are combined into one global awareness.

With athletes of the mind, internal martial artists share the paradox that in order to activate the shen, they must use the yi to stop the yi. First, both learn to use the yi to sustain relaxation for long periods of time. This prolongs the systemic parasympathetic stimulation of both the motor and sensory components by the hypothalamic core. Eventually, when maintained for too long a time, a threshold is reached and a crisis results. "Spillover" occurs and the hypothalamic cortex floods the sensory-motor system with sympathetic nervous system stimulation. The moment spillover occurs and maximal sympathetic stimulation is simultaneous with maximal parasympathetic stimulation, the experience peaks and becomes transcendent. The functions of the frontal lobe, including the yi, shut down. There is no ego, no intent, no planning, no past, no future; time contracts into the now of the present moment of crisis and the sensory-motor system experiences a tremendous surge of energy.

For both the athletes of the mind and the internal martial artists, the general feeling of well being produced by the primary parasympathetic activation is intensified by the systemic sympathetic stimulation into heightened experiences of euphoria and ecstasy. The sympathetic surge also hyper-prepares the motor system for action. The individual not only experiences feelings of great power and invulnerability but in fact becomes capable of enormous strength and agility. Indeed, this is the moment of truth for his training. All the faps he worked so hard to acquire and internalize now operate effortlessly and execute flawlessly while successfully meeting the challenges presented by the crisis.

The shen of internal martial artists, in common with the shen of the mystics of the body including the external martial arts, consists of the unfiltered contents of the parietal lobe, i.e., the totality of perceptual data of all the senses perceived simultaneously. Indeed, in this augmented awareness that is shen, the very distinction between foreground and background disappears. What is special about the shen of the internal martial arts is that in addition to the simultaneity in awareness of foreground and background, there is simultaneous awareness of a third realm of being, namely the inner ground. In this highest state of enlightened perceptual awareness, the background, the foreground and the inner ground combine simultaniously into the holistic awareness that is the shen of the internal martial artist (Fig. 44).

Fig. 44
The Three Grounds of Being

Cultivating the inner ground is of course the very essence of standing meditation. We cultivate awareness of the inter-connections between our internal components and their effect on the overall balance of the body as a whole. Balance and proprioceptive senses, being largely controlled by the cerebellum, therefore usually operate on a sub-conscious level of awareness. But in standing meditation the yi, or intent, cultivates the internal awareness of balance and the integration of the parts of the body. In turn, this helps to improve and fine-tune cerebellar functioning by simplifying and minimizing its work load and increasing efficiency.

Standing meditation, the forms, tuishou and other faps of the internal martial arts integrate the internal senses of balance and proprioception with the background and foreground senses of vision and touch in a systematic, interactive, responsiveness training. In fact, the range of interactive movements of the tuishou practices coincides precisely with the range of the peri-personal space mapped by the parietal lobes (Fig. 45). Or, to put it a different way: the very purpose of tuishou practice is the training of awareness and responsiveness within peri-personal space in which both touch and vision are critically important.

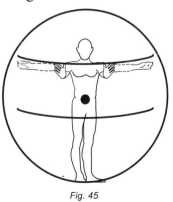

Fig. 45
Peri personal Space

This fact is beginning to be recognized by contemporary writers on brain science. Blakeslee & Blakeslee write, "The martial art tai chi is a graceful and elegant way to explore your [peri]personal space. [It] is like learning a language, only it is the language of body and space in motion. The goal is total unification of mind, body, and intention."[83]

As the internal martial arts cultivate the lightness of enlightened touch, an internal artist's mastery of peri-personal space expands until he is untouchable on defense and unstoppable on offense. Untouchable on defense–because in his yielding he has become so soft, light and elusive that while he gives his opponent the point of contact, that opponent cannot find a point to apply force. Unstoppable in offense–because in the lightness of his touch, he is able to work below the radar of an opponent's perception and thus use his softness to elicit the opponent's involuntary frame, capture his center and then dispose of him as desired. Often, during demonstrations exhibiting total control over his opponents, Master Tam will joke and tease them, "Now our two bodies are united as one, but, unfortunately for you, it's my mind that is controlling them."

For the internal martial arts, the experience of the shen state can happen either as a result of long arduous training or in actual martial encounter. Whatever the context, the first time, it will always come unexpectedly as a total surprise. As the occurrences of shen go from the sporadic to more frequent, the experience becomes more repeatable and predictable. In other words, shen, too, is a learned skill. In time, the internal martial artist finds it easier and easier to slip voluntarily into this state. The great ones, like Master Tam, seem to be permanently in this state of total awareness of the peri-personal space surrounding them.

---

[83] Sandra Blakeslee & Matthew Blakeslee, *"The Body has a Mind of its Own,"* Random House, New York, 2008, p.133.

Chapter 10: The Elightenment of the Internal Martial Artist

Shen and Enlightenment

The question arises: What is the relationship between shen, this sublime spirit of awareness, and enlightenment? And what exactly do we mean by enlightenment? A clue may be found in the name of the student organization associated with many of Master Tam's public appearances in seminars and retreats. In Chinese, it is written:

Kang1

Le4

Nei4

Jia1

Quan2

She4

Since the formation of this organization, Master Tam's English translation of these Chinese characters has consistently been "The Internal Martial Arts Association for Health and Enlightenment" (IMAAHE) and the characters and translation have graced the organization's literature and website. However, when we look at common dictionary translations of the root meaning of these characters, we see a slightly different emphasis. From top to bottom, we have: kang1 (health, healthy); le4 (happy, happiness); nei4 (inner, inside, internal); jia1 (family, household, "school" as in "school of thought"); quan2 (fist, boxing); she4 (society, organization). The greatest difference, obviously, lies in the common rendering of le4 as "happiness," whereas Master Tam renders it as "enlightenment." On the surface, to a westerner, these meanings may seem too far apart to be translations of the same word. But actually, there is a large congruence and area of overlap, so that an alternate, and also correct, translation of the characters would be "Internal Martial Arts Association for Health and Happiness."

What then, is the connection between the two? Happiness is largely an affair of the heart and the enlightenment talked about here refers to the heart. When we are unhappy, we have a heavy heart; when we are happy, we are light hearted.

Therefore, to the extent that we are happier, our hearts become lighter—and not only lighter, but enlightened. This also clarifies at once the relationship between shen and enlightenment. For whereas shen pertains to the enlightenment of the senses in an expanded perceptual awareness, enlightenment (le4), as the term is used by Master Tam and IMAAHE, pertains to the realm of feelings and the heart, about how we are feeling about our lives and the world around us.

It's quite possible, therefore to be enlightened in the sense of happiness (le4) without having the expanded perceptual awareness of shen. The internal martial arts practitioner whose main purpose is simply health can certainly achieve happiness/enlightenment of the heart before he attains the state of shen. But since the shen level represents the apex of any art, including the internal martial arts, when you have the shen, you already will have kang le, that is, you will be enlightened through happiness, and then the shen will in turn deepen and enrich the kang le.

The choice of the English term *enlightenment* is fortuitous in that it provides an apt metaphor to chart the progression of the internal martial artist and in so doing recapitulates and summarizes the main points of this volume. In English "light" enters into several polarity structures, most notably light/dark and light/heavy. Together these two polarity structures and their derivatives are expressive of two of the most basic forces of nature, light (luminance) and gravity. As such they provide an internally consistent metaphorical framework of description of the internal martial artist's body/mind training towards enlightenment (Fig. 46).

Fig. 46
The Dual Nature
of Enlightenment

The Enlightenment of the Body/Mind

For the internal martial artist, enlightenment is a process that proceeds from the physical to the mental. The enlightenment of the body is a prerequisite for the enlightenment of the mind. The enlightenment of the body begins with posture; enlightened posture in turn enables enlightened movement. Next, this enlightened movement is guided and directed by enlightened perceptual awareness. This enlightened perceptual awareness enables us to engage in enlightened interactivity as expressive of the enlightened heart.

Enlightenment as a gravity metaphor, based on the light/heavy polarity, applies to the bodily, somatic aspects of bone, tendon and muscle and their integration in balanced posture and movement. In other words, the enlightenment of the body begins with refining and redefining our relationship to gravity.

The enlightenment of the body is first and foremost the enlightenment of its posture through standing meditation. Based on six-direction oppositional relaxation and exertion, standing meditation develops awareness of both central equilibrium and the relationships of the body's parts to each other; these two are the foundational senses for the enlightenment of posture.

As the body posture becomes optimally aligned with gravity, it takes less and less energy to maintain it and therefore the body becomes both lighter and more stable. In realigning the body parts optimally with respect to gravity, standing meditation integrates the body's matrix of muscle, bone and connective tissue into an elastic structural frame of the zhengti (整體), or coherent body.

When the enlightened posture is maintained in movement, enlightened movement results. Internal martial arts movement training is an extension of postural training. Likewise based on oppositional relaxation and exertion in the six directions, the enlightened movement that results is as agile as the enlightened posture is stable. The body literally feels and moves ever more lightly, becoming so responsive as to eventually achieve a state of permanent lightness that seems to defy gravity. Enlightened movement first becomes fluid, like water. Then it becomes like the wind. In time it seems to move without moving, being suddenly here, then suddenly there, until the movement is below the threshold of normal perception.

In short, internal martial arts training is the ongoing process of combining ever greater postural stability with ever greater movement agility, and it is this control over gravity that constitutes the enlightenment of the body. On the one hand, six-direction training in stillness makes the body so strong and stable as to be one with the earth and immovable, apparently increasing or even merging with the force of gravity. On the other hand, six-direction training in movement makes the body so light as to seemingly decrease or even defy the force of gravity.

As the enlightenment of the body makes use of the gravity metaphor, so the enlightenment of the mind makes use of the electro-magnetic (light) metaphor that is based on the light/dark polarity. Awareness, knowledge, wisdom and goodness are light, as opposed to the darkness of ignorance and evil. Enlightenment in this sense can refer to either the process of light triumphing over darkness or the resulting state of being.

...

In as much as yi and shen are the mental aspects that control the somatic functions of balance and integration in enlightened posture and movement, the enlightenment of the perceptual mind occurs with the transition of yi into shen. How so? Yi, by its ability to focus, excludes and eliminates most of the surrounding world from the field of perception, and it is precisely the totality of sensory information excluded by the yi that constitutes the content of the shen and its spirit of awareness.

In the moment of transcendence, the frontal lobe (yi) and its focusing function are inhibited, allowing awareness to expand to and include the totality of parietal sensory information, not just of one sense, but of all the senses. When the veil of darkness of non-awareness is lifted and the doors of perception are fully opened, all perceptual modalities are simultaneously integrated into shen.

From the purely martial point of view, this global, simultaneous awareness makes shen even faster than yi in responding to stimuli. In the movement of its focus from one object to another, the yi creates a sequence, a timeline of consideration of objects that does not exist in the simultaneity of shen awareness. Shen allows a simultaneous response to a stimulus.

For martial artists, the second great advantage of the shen level over the yi, is that while the yi uses the body's power to control an opponent, the shen has the ability to use no-force, the enlightened touch, to accomplish its aim.

...

Once, in Barcelona, I had the opportunity to observe how Master Tam's shen state gives him an amazingly consistent 360 degrees of spatial awareness. As we strolled

down Las Ramblas, I happened to be walking behind him and I watched as a pickpocket tried with a deft touch to reach into his pocket from behind (Fig. 47). Without breaking stride Master Tam simply turned his body a bit and, slowly raising his arms a little, caused his would-be robber to lose balance. Master Tam was smiling the whole time, even as the pickpocket disappeared into the crowd. The movement was so relaxed and the timing so perfect that it looked as if it had been rehearsed to perfection.

Fig. 47
The Pickpocket

At workshops, also, I have seen countless demonstrations that Master Tam is as aware of what is happening in back of him as of what's going on in front. For example, in the eagerness to test his abilities, at times a student steps over the line of good manners and cannot resist the temptation to try and push him unexpectedly from behind. Inevitably, he senses the attempt and deals with it in the customary manner. He yields to the opponent's pressure and uses it to capture and immobilize him or to bounce him away.

Enlightened Touch + Enlightened Heart = Enlightened Interaction

Since the internal martial arts ultimately are interactive, any claims of enlightenment of the body must be judged within the context of the ability to resolve physical conflict by entering into an enlightened manner of interaction with other bodies. The dimension of enlightenment we speak of here occurs in the tactile realm of touch and pressure. As we have seen, this goes to the very essence of the internal martial arts.

The successful cultivation of an ever lighter and lighter touch is the enlightenment that allows the internal martial artist to capture and control the opponent's center through the use of awareness and no-force.

But before skills of lightness and no-force can be acquired, they must be desired; there must be a change of heart that amounts to an enlightenment of the heart. Indeed, enlightenment of the heart and enlightenment of the touch are deeply intertwined. Enlightenment of the heart is a prerequisite for enlightenment of the sense of touch and enlightenment of the touch begets deeper enlightenment of the heart.

Master Tam's own story is living proof of this point. When he was a young man in his fighting years, Master Tam had a quite low opinion of taijiquan and was very unimpressed by most of the practitioners he had met; in his opinion, they talked a lot, way too much in fact, and could not back up their claims for taijiquan's superiority. In numerous interactions, he confirmed that without exception he could beat them easily with his Eagle Claw or with other martial arts systems he knew.

In later years, Master Tam described the reasons for the change of heart that came over him:

> We are here on this planet in order to get along. So that made me think a lot about the limitations of the use of force as a method of exercising control of one's situation.

> I was respected and feared, but not that well liked. And although I never hurt anyone, people feared my skills ... I found out that flaunting your strength and using force don't make you any friends.

> The use of force and strength by the external martial arts to control a situation will ultimately turn a friend into an enemy, where as the mastery of softness and awareness of internal martial arts will almost immediately turn an enemy into a friend.[84]

---

[84] Jan Diepersloot, "*The Tao of Yiquan: The Method of Awareness in the Martial Arts,*" Qi Works, Walnut Creek, 1999, p. 212.

Master Tam once recounted a trigger event that spurred his determination to master the lightness that is the most sublime expression of the internal martial arts. On the occasion of a big martial arts dinner, a respected teacher remarked about him that "while his (Master Tam's) gongfu is so good as to make him unbeatable, his taiji is not there yet." Hearing these words affected Master Tam deeply. They stirred in him the realization that his martial arts journey was not yet complete and that the greatest challenges might still lie ahead.

This story also illustrates the decisive role the shifu (teacher or respected elder), plays in the successful transmission of the internal martial arts from one generation to the next. The main influences on Master Tam's process of evolution were Professor Yu Pengxi (尤彭熙) from the yiquan system and Dr. Qi Jiangtao（綦江濤）, the taiji master. Dr. Qi especially, transmitted to him the moral philosophy of the taiji principle incorporated in the strategy and techniques of yielding. Professor Yu, who transmitted the theory and training methods for the soft power of internal martial arts to him, also counseled him to take the time to develop and master the art on his own and not go out in public until he had done so.

Master Tam understood that it would require patience and perseverance on his part to give up all his old ways of using strength while retraining himself in the soft power of the taiji principle. The consolidation of this inner change and enlightenment of the heart, and its outer expression in the enlightened touch, would not only be a life changing process, but also a time-consuming affair. Master Tam, therefore, heeded the words of his teacher, and withdrew from the world.

That was in the late 1980s, when Master Tam was in his 50s. With this self-imposed seclusion, he acted very much in keeping with the Chinese tradition going back to Chuang Tzu, Tamo and others. In this tradition, illumination and insight as a student is followed by a period of seclusion during which mastery is achieved and after which one emerges publicly as a teacher.

For those of us in the San Francisco Bay Area who for years had seen Master Tam on a regular basis, nearly seven years passed before he began to re-emerge in public and to teach.

An enlightened heart leads to an enlightened mind and we trust an enlightened person as someone who has first and foremost dispelled the darkness of his own confusion and ignorance. The moral and ethical dimensions of enlightenment are inextricably intertwined with the cognitive dimension. Just as good and evil are metaphorically associated with light and dark, so are knowledge and ignorance. Being able to "shed light" on things and illuminate the path, Master Tam has helped, and continues to help, hundreds of his students and other fellow human beings by providing conceptual clarity, wisdom and insight not only into the human condition in general, but also into one's individual problems.

Enlightened Transmission

Master Tam began his teaching in the San Francisco Bay Area, but soon he was conducting workshops and retreats in the United States, Europe, the Middle East and Asia. As his reputation spread worldwide, it became his turn not only to carry on the tradition of shifu, but also to become recognized as one of the world's greatest authorities on the internal martial arts.

As part and parcel of this reality, a steady and increasing stream of visitors from all over the world has come knocking at his door, seeking individual training, instruction and counseling. Many, if not most, of these visitors are already teachers of martial arts and in fact come to Master Tam to learn his style with the intent of teaching it.

Though he has not sought out this recognition, the process has made Master Tam a de facto "teacher of teachers." In Chinese, there is a term for this: dashi (大師), an honorific bestowed strictly on the basis of skill and actual achievement. Da meaning "big" and "shi" meaning "teacher", dashi (大師) literally means "Big Teacher." The dashi is a purveyor of enlightenment, sought out by other teachers who desire to receive the deepest knowledge and acquire the most refined skills.

The atmosphere Master Tam creates among the participants in his workshops and retreats clearly showcases his mastery of the enlightened touch and the enlightened heart. Force begets force, and only the skill of the enlightened soft touch, as the expression of the enlightened heart, ultimately has the power to soften a hardened heart and literally turn a heavy-handed situation into a light-hearted one.

In workshops, one of Master Tam's favorite pedagogic tools is to explain the way of the internal martial arts as the necessity of confronting and coming to terms with our "dark side" or the "evil twin." He will pick out someone who is exhibiting an excessive desire to "get people" and, alluding to similarities to himself in a previous era, he will jokingly refer to this individual as his "evil twin." In the demonstration that follows Master Tam urges the person to attack him, and then gives an object lesson in why the aggressive approach is self-defeating and the yielding approach is superior. Then, for good measure, he sometimes calls on one of the smaller and more timid people to come out, and by just guiding that person's movement very gently, he enables the disarming and control of the bigger and more aggressive person. Inevitably, this amazes and amuses the participants and the observers alike.

Indeed, as master of the enlightened touch and the enlightened heart, Master Tam creates an unending stream of humorous situations in his workshops, and in doing so, promotes good feeling and high spirits in the proceedings. Frequently, in pushing hands with Master Tam, one has the experience of being controlled by nothing more substantial than the spirit of awareness. For some reason, perhaps its inherent paradoxical nature, it is often incongruously funny and engenders a shared light-heartedness in both the controller and the controlled. As anyone who has ever attended one of Master Tam's workshops can attest, this process works every time, without fail. Master Tam takes all comers, and from the most eager to believe to the most cynical, the response is always identical; a slow, incredulous smile spreads across their lips, invariably followed by the question, "Would you do that again?"

...

As an example of the profound way Master Tam has influenced the lives of so many students worldwide, I would like to conclude this volume by telling the story I know most intimately: my own. I would like to share how Master Tam helped me to have that change of heart and how that helped lead me to greater happiness and enlightenment in my life as well as my art.

I began my studies with Master Tam in the late 1990s. The first five years or so after Master Tam accepted me as a student were very exciting indeed. Giving up previous forms and meditations to embrace Master Tam's, I learned many new forms and many tuishou patterns. I both thought and felt that I was embracing his teachings and instructions wholeheartedly and that I was progressing rapidly.

The next five years were less happy. I began to notice, for example, that despite the excitement of learning all the new forms and techniques, in the actual mastery of the essence of the art, I wasn't progressing as fast as I had anticipated. Often, also, after visiting Master Tam for private instructions I came home in a mixed-up emotional state, awed and inspired by what I had been privileged to witness on the one hand and yet disheartened and frustrated with my lack of progress. Moreover, the truth was dawning on me that after years of instruction and practice, the skills of enlightened touch and soft force still eluded me; I remained in the dark, caught in a web of inner contradictions. Finally, after some 10 years of study, a watershed event occurred in which I was forced to confront my own dark shadow. This confrontation proved to be the turning point in my enlightenment process.

With the benefit of hindsight, it is easy to see what was happening. New conscious desires and old unconscious habits and impulses were in conflict. Consciously I was committed to the principle of no resistance and my desire was to learn how to yield in order not to lose. But this outward and conscious acceptance of the philosophy of yielding served to hide the deeper truth of my inner contradiction: an unconscious resistance to the practice of yielding and a desire to win even if it meant using force.

This inner contradiction in my approach to the art also entailed a growing contradictory relationship with my teacher. My conscious mind was following Master Tam, but my heart was not, and this divergence from the true path represented an abandonment of his teachings. In truth, on a subconscious level, I was far from wholeheartedly embracing his teachings; internally, a large core of resistance in me kept fighting against them.

This was clearly manifest in my pushing hands play. In the early days of his teaching, Master Tam exclusively emphasized the defensive, yielding aspects of the patterns and forms of tuishou. But rather than mastering yielding, rather than mastering responsiveness and the no-force of yielding defensively, I began using the tuishou techniques I learned offensively, to *win*, even if that meant using force. In this, I was not only reversing the priorities set by my teacher, but I was abandoning the very principle of taiji, which is using no-force to defeat force.

...

Master Tam, of course, was more aware of these things going on inside me than I was myself, and throughout the years he patiently tried to redirect me in the right direction, to little avail. Then, sometime in 2006 or 2007, he decided that since his gentle prodding had proved ineffective, sterner measures were required.

We were having our customary late afternoon coffee in the neighborhood café. After some initial pleasantries, he looked me in the eyes and calmly and somewhat emphatically remarked that it was time "to put the cards on the table" (Fig. 48). He proceeded to skillfully puncture the balloon of my self-image by laying bare my inner contradictions. It was a dressing down that

Fig. 48
Being Shown the Errors of my Way

opened doors because it opened my eyes. He compelled me to look in the mirror and to recognize and accept the naked truth: despite superficial appearances in my pursuit of the art, I was violating its basic tenets.

He made me see how I was using ambition and force to pursue my opponents and defeat them, rather than waiting patiently for the opportunity to come to me and controlling my opponents by yielding to their force. He pointed out how I was using substitute methods, such as skillful leaning, using hand force and partial strength, for short term benefit at the expense of the true, principled method that would take longer to pay off, but would deliver a bigger return. To drive home his view that we should give up short-term gain and go for long-term accomplishment, he used the metaphor that in our progress, we should grow like the trunk of a tree and not like the side branches. The trunk grows slower but will reach the greatest height, while the side branch will grow fast at first, but then slow to a halt.

I realized this was a seminal moment. I wasn't getting any younger. This was the last chance, perhaps a split in the road, and either choice involved a surrender, one positive and one negative. If I wanted what he had to offer and to maintain the possibility of realizing my dream, then I would have to surrender to his teaching, start listening to him and without question carry out the letter and spirit of his instructions. Or I could surrender to my own dark side, walk away and give up my dream of excellence and mastery of the art, defeated by my own false pride.

Framed in that perspective, I had no choice. I had to stop fighting my teacher, my opponents and myself. I had to stop fighting *period*. To stop fighting meant to start accepting. Not resisting, but accepting and following Master Tam's instructions; not resisting, but accepting my opponent's force; not resisting, but accepting myself and my true potential. Listening to his words, I finally took them to heart and that change of heart led in turn to my beginning access to the enlightened touch and enlightened interaction.

...

As of this writing, it has been some half dozen years since Master Tam forced me to confront my dark side. Since then, I'm happy to report, the course correction he provoked in me has enabled me to achieve modest skill in the "mysteries" of yielding and soft power.

My experience during this time has verified to me that, for the internal martial artist, enlightenment begins and ends with the heart. It begins when the enlightened heart enables the body to become enlightened through the true alignment of its posture and movement.

After the wakeup call, I became very strict with myself. Especially when pushing hands, I had to foreswear any impulse to initiate an attack. It did not take long before a cascade of beneficial changes began to happen in many different areas. It was as if all the pieces had been there all along, but had been prevented from falling into place by my own excesses of intent.

The more I became successful during tuishou encounters in setting aside everything pertaining to winning–all thoughts and intentions, instincts and desires–the more all the issues that had been giving me problems–issues of central equilibrium and zhengti, of timing in the responsiveness skills–began to resolve themselves. First I found that restraining my excessively proactive tendencies was key in progressing toward a more enlightened posture. Why and how? Because in actively searching for opportunities to apply force to the opponent I had developed the habit of leaning forward, constantly compromising my central equilibrium and causing me to use partial, as opposed to wholistic, force.

The improvement in my central equilibrium began to resolve outstanding issues of body integration. Being more habitually upright, the alignment of the spine at both ends allows the body parts to cohere and integrate more fully. Adjustment in the lumbar curve allowed my lower trunk to integrate and cohere more fully with the upper trunk above, and with the foundation of the legs below. Adjustment in the cervical curve allowed better integration and coherence of the head with the torso. Keeping my hands and arms, so busy previously searching for openings to attack, calm and receptive, they began to really feel like extensions of my center. Thus, all my separate body parts began to fall into place and hang together, uniting themselves ever more concretely into the zhengti, the coherent, enlightened body.

As the three dimensions/six directions orientational polarities became experiential realities, they more and more became functional variables at my disposal in dealing with an opponent in pushing hands. Increasingly, I experienced the truth that the left and right sides, the front and back sides, the upper and lower halves of my body, must cooperate in the maintenance of central equilibrium by opposing each other. Learning to balance the opposing directions of each dimension, these orientational polarities have become the foundation for the shape-shifting of my sphere and frame in movement and responsiveness training.

The discipline of not attacking helped me to acquire more patience. If I couldn't go after my opponent, I had no choice but to be ready, waiting to let him make the first move. This patience taught me that not having any intention, but paying full attention, is the basis for developing true responsiveness in the skills of listening, following, yielding and sticking. Why? As long as you have an intention to do something, your attention is occupied and not available to "listen" to your opponent, and respond to him in the moment.

In other words, when you have an intention or your attention is otherwise occupied, there will always be a time delay between the stimulus and the involuntary reaction that follows it; when you have intention and your opponent makes a move against you, you can only react involuntarily. Therefore, before we can respond voluntarily and simultaneously to our opponent's initiative, we must let go of all intention and embrace our opponent with our full attention. Only when we pay full attention to an opponent can we achieve the simultaneity in timing between stimulus and response that defines the enlightened interaction as the essence of the internal martial arts.

...

In the final analysis, enlightenment is always relative, whether compared to one's own previous state or to the achievements of others. Compared with Master Tam, my level of enlightenment is like the early dawn of day and his, high noon. But compared to the darkness of my previous state, now the true nature of the art is—and continues to become—much clearer.

Yet because many details still remain to be illuminated and because there is neither a limit nor an end to the subtlety of these arts, as long as I am capable I will remain a passionate student, continually striving to expand my insight and perfect my skill.

Then, because I have been shown the way forward and handed a torch, my mission, too, has become one of transmission. Being able to spend my remaining years passing on this deep and wonderful art continues to make each one more than golden for me, a priceless and profound sense of personal completion. For my life now is the fulfillment of an epiphany many years ago that started me on this quest. Indeed, so significant was this event in my life that the very memory of it, for better or worse, makes me break out in verse:

It was December 1974,
so down and out I could take no more
tied in knots, at the end of my rope
I had no illusions and no hope

Attending a taiji demonstration
lighting struck, a blinding realization,
'tis not too late! I can recast my fate!
and saw my future self as he was meant to be

That old man in the park, still with that spark,
slowing into tranquility, yet growing in ability,
making his mark, bringing light to dark
after the vision, the decision: the die was cast, I threw off the past

The journey was rough, the going tough
many hurdles, detours to nowhere
but keeping to the turtle, never the hare
I followed my bliss and it came to this:

Today, here's the old fart, passing on the art,
with gusto and heart, still dancing creation,
what blessing, what elation
delivering the goods to the next generation.

Appendices
Chinese Characters Used

WORDS		
Characters	**Pinyin**	**English**
八段錦	ba duan gin	eight Brocades
百會	baihui	point on the head
黐手	chi sao	sticky hands
丹田	dantian	abdominal center
導引	daoyin	exercise
大師	dashi	teacher of teachers
功夫	gongfu	skill
後天氣	houtian qi	post-birth qi
勁	jin	martial power
精	jing	essential energy
肌肉若一	ji rou ruo yi	the muscles as one
毛髮如戟	mao fa ru ji	hair like halberds
命門	mingmen	point on lower back
內家 拳	neijia quan	Internal martial arts family
氣	qi	energy
氣功	qigong	health exercise
神	shen	spirit
師弟	shidi	younger brother
師父	Shifu	teacher
收即是放	shou ji shi fang	to gather in is to release
鬆	song	relaxed
太極	taiji	primordial principle
太極拳	taijiquan	"ultimate principle" martial art
聽	ting	listening
推手	tuishou	pushing hands
無極	wuji	the void, stillness

無為	wuwei	non-doing
先天氣	xiantian qi	pre-birth qi
洗髓經	xi sui jing	bone marrow cleansing classic
陽	yang	active
意	yi	intent
易筋經	yi jin jing	muscle/tendon changing classic
陰	yin	passive
粘 黏	zhan-nian	adhering/sticking
整體	zhengti	coherent body
志	zhi	will
中定	zhongding	central equilibrium
走	zou	yielding
NAMES		
譚曼彥	Tam Maan Yin	
劉法孟	Liu Fameng	
張驤伍	Zhang Xiang Wu	
常東昇	Chang Dongsheng	
韓星垣	Han Xingyuan	
尤彭熙	Yu Pengxi	
綦江濤	Qi Jiangtao	
蔡松芳	Cai Songfang	
庖丁	Pao Ding	
莊子	Zhuangzi	
王薌齋	Wang Xiangzhai	
鄭曼青	Zheng Manqing	
楊露禪	Yang Luchan	
吳光明	Kuang-Ming Wu	

List of Illustrations

Works Consulted

Internal Martial Arts

Bracy, John & Xing-Han Liu, "*Ba Gua: Hidden Knowledge in the Taoist Internal Martial Art*", North Atlantic Books, Berkeley, CA, 1998.

Braverman, Arthur, trans., "*Warrior of Zen: The Diamond-hard Wisdom Mind of Suzuki Shosan*", Kodansha International, New York, Tokyo, London, 1994.

Chen, Y.K., "*Tai-Chi Ch'uan: Its Effects and Practical Applications*", Newcastle Publishing Co., Inc., North Hollywood, CA, 1979.

Clark, Angus, "*The Complete Illustrated Guide to Tai Chi: A Practical Approach to the Ancient Chinese Movement for Health and Well-Being*", Element Books Ltd., Boston, MA, 2000.

Davis, Barbara, ed., "*Chen Weiming: Taiji Sword and other Writings*", North Atlantic Books, Berkeley, CA, 2000.

Durckheim, Karlfried Graf, "*Hara: The Vital Center of Man*", Inner Traditions, Rochester, Vermont, 1956.

Frantzis, Bruce, "*Tai Chi Health for Life: Why it Works for Health, Stress Relief and Longevity*", Energy Arts, Inc. and Blue Snake Books, Fairfax, CA and Berkeley, CA, 2003.

Frantzis, B.K., "*The Power of Internal Martial Arts: Combat Secrets of Ba Gua, Tai Chi and Hsing-I*", North Atlantic Books, Berkeley, CA, 1998.

Frantzis, B.K., "*Opening the Energy Gates of Your Body: Gain Lifelong Vitality*", North Atlantic Books, Berkeley, CA, 1993.

Fu Zhongwen, "*Mastering Yang Style Taijiquan*", Louis Swaim, trans., North Atlantic Books, Berkeley, CA,1999.

Ha, Fong, "*Yiquan and the Nature of Energy: The Fine Art of Doing Nothing and Achieving Everything*", Summerhouse Publications, Berkeley, CA, 1998.

Huang Wen-Shan, "*Fundamentals of Tai Chi Ch'uan*", South Sky Book Company, Hong Kong, 1973.

Hyams, Joe, "*Zen in the Martial Arts*", J.P. Tarcher, Inc., Los Angeles, CA, 1979.

Jin, Yunting, ed., "*The Xingyi Boxing Manual: Hebei Style's Five Principles and Seven Words*", North Atlantic Books, Berkeley, CA, 2004.

Klein, Bob, "*Movements of Magic: The Spirit of T'ai-Chi-Ch'uan*", Newcastle Publishing Co., Inc., North Hollywood, CA, 1984.

Kobayashi, Petra and Toyo, "*Classical T'ai Chi Sword*", Tuttle Publishing, Boston, 2003.

Lee,Ying-Arng, "*The Secret Arts of Chinese Leg Manoeuvres in Pictures*", Unicorn Press, Hong Kong, 1962.

Liao, Waysun, "*T'ai Chi Classics: New Translations of Three Essential Texts of Tai Chi Ch'uan*", Shambhala, Boston & London, 1990.

Licht, Jurgen, ed., "*Seven Treasures of Taijiquan*", Jurgen Licht, Munich, Germany, 2001.

Lowenthal, Wolfe, "*There Are No Secrets: Prof. Cheng Man-Ch'ing and his Tai Chi Chuan*",
North Atlantic Books, Berkeley, CA, 1991.

Lowenthal, Wolfe, "*Gateway to the Miraculous: Further Explorations in the Tao of Cheng Man-ch'ing*",
Frog, Ltd., Berkeley, CA, 1994.

Lu, Shengli, "*Combat Techniques of Taiji, Xingyi, and Bagua: Principles and Practices of Internal Martial Arts*", Blue Snake Books, Berkeley, CA, 2006.

Ma, Yueh-liang & Wen Zee, "*Wu Style Tai Chi Chuan Tuishou (Push-Hands)*",
Shanghai Book Co., Ltd., Hong Kong, 1986.

Maisel, Edward, "*Tai Chi for Health*", Holt, Rinehart and Winston, New York, 1972.

Miller, Dan & Cartmell, Tim, eds., "*Xing Yi Nei Gong: Xing Yi Health Maintenance and Internal Strength Development*", High View Publications, Pacific Grove, CA, 1994.

Ming, Shi, "*Mind over Matter: Higher Martial Arts*", Frog, Ltd., Berkeley, CA, 1994.

Nagaboshi, Tomio, "*The Bodhisattva Warriors: The Origin, Inner Philosophy, History and Symbolism of the Buddhist Martial Art Within India and China*", Samuel Weiser, Inc., York Beach, Maine, 1994.

Olson, Stuart Alve, "*Steal My Art: The Life and Times of T'ai Chi Master T.T. Liang*",
North Atlantic Books, Berkeley, CA, 2002.

Olson, Stuart Alve, trans., "*The Wind Sweeps Away The Plum Blossoms: The Principles and Techniques of the Yang Style T'ai Chi Spear and Staff*", Bubbling-Well Press, Manitoba, Canada, 1985.

Petersen, Stephen P., PhD, "*The Quantum Tai Chi Gauge Theory: The Dance of Mind Over Matter*",
Empyrean Quest Publishers, Concord, CA, 1996.

Pittman, Allen, "*Pa-Kua: Eight-Trigram Boxing*", Charles E. Tuttle Company, Inc.,
Rutland, Vermont & Tokyo, Japan, 1990.

Ralston, Peter, "*The Art of Effortless Power*", North Atlantic Books, Berkeley, CA, 1991.

Ralston, Peter, "*Cheng Hsin: The Principles of Effortless Power*", North Atlantic Books, Berkeley, CA, 1989.

Reid, Howard & Croucher, Michael, "*The Way of the Warrior: The Paradox of the Martial Arts*",
Leopard Books, London, 1995.

Reid, Howard, "*The Way of Harmony: A Guide to Self-Knowledge Through the Arts of T'ai Chi Chuan, Hsing I, Pa Kua, and Chi Kung*", Simon & Schuster Inc., New York, 1988.

Sawai, Kenichi, "*Taiki-Ken: The Essence of Kung-fu*", Japan Publications, Inc., Elmsford, NY, 1976.

Smith, Robert W., "*Martial Musings: A Portrayal of Martial Arts in the 20th Century*",
Via Media Publishing Company, Erie, Pennsylvania, 1999.

Smith, Robert W., "*Hsing-I: Chinese Mind-Body Boxing*", Kodansha International, Tokyo,
New York & San Francisco, 1974.

Smith, Robert W., "*Chinese Boxing: Masters and Methods*", North Atlantic Books, Berkeley, CA, 1974.

Smith, Robert W., "*Pa-Kua: Chinese Boxing for Fitness and Self-Defense*", Kodansha International Ltd.,
Tokyo, Japan & Palo Alto, CA, 1967.

Smith, Robert W., ed., *"Secrets of Shaolin Temple Boxing"*, Charles E. Tuttle Company, Inc., Rutland, Vermont & Tokyo, Japan, 1964.

Sun, Lu Tang, *"Xing Yi Quan Xue: The Study of Form-Mind Boxing"*, High View Publications, Pacific Grove, CA, 1993.

Sykes, S.L., *"Stanford Researchers Record 'Optimal Force' of Tai Chi Master"*, Mercury News, San Jose, CA., 5//3/07.

Tackett, Tim, *"Hsing-I Kung-fu, Volume II: Combat"*, Ohara Publications, Inc., Burbank, CA, 1963.

Tohei, Koichi, *"Book of Ki: Co-ordinating Mind and Body in Daily Life"*, Japan Publications, Inc., Tokyo, Japan, 1976.

Ueshiba, Kisshomaru, *"The Spirit of Aikido"*, Kodansha International, Tokyo, 1984.

Wang, Xuanjie, *"Dachengquan"*, Hai Feng Publishing Co., Ltd., Hong Kong, 1988.

Wang, Xuanjie, *"Dacheng Kungfu: The Truth of Chinese Martial Art"*, China Prospect Publishing House & Shanghai Book Co., Ltd., Hong Kong, 1989.

Wang, Xiangzhai, *"The Right Path of Yiquan"*, Li Jong & T. Hekkila, trans., ebooks, 2001.

Wang, Xiangzhai, *"The Essence of Martial Art: The Theory of Yiquan"*, Li Jong & T. Hekkila trans., ebooks, 2001.

Wells, Marnix, *"Scholar Boxer: Chang Naizhou's Theory of Internal Martial Arts and the Evolution of Taijiquan"*, North Atlantic Books, Berkeley, CA, 2005.

Westbrook, A., & Jue, Ratti O., *"Aikido and the Dynamic Sphere: An Illustrated Introduction"*, Charles E. Tuttle Company, Rutland, Vermont, 1970.

Wile, Douglas ed., *"Master Cheng's Thirteen Chapters On T'ai Chi Ch'uan"*, Sweet Ch'i Press, NY, NY, 1982.

Wile, Douglas ed., *"T'ai-chi Touchstones: Yang Family Secret Transmissions"*, Sweet Ch'i Press, NY, NY, 1983.

Wile, Douglas ed., *"Lost T'ai-Chi Classics from the Late Ch'ing Dynasty"*, State University of New York Press, Albany, New York, 1996.

Wile, Douglas, ed., *"Chen Man-Ch'ing's Advanced T'ai-Chi Form Instructions: With Selected Writings on Meditation, the I Ching, Medicine and the Arts"*, Sweet Ch'i Press, New York, 1985.

Yang, Jwing-Ming, Dr., *"Advanced Yang Style Tai Chi Chuan V. 1: Tai Chi Theory and Tai Chi Jing"*, Yang's Martial Arts Association, Jamaica Plain, MA, 1987.

Yang, Jwing-Ming & Dr. Shou-Yu Liang, *"Hsing Yi Chuan: Theory and Applications"*, Yang's Martial Arts Association, Hong Kong, 1990.

Zhang, Yun & Lu Shengli, *"Combat Techniques of Taiji, Xingyi, and Bagua: Principles and Practices of Internal Martial Arts"*, Blue Snake Books, Berkeley, CA, 2006.

Anatomy, Physiology and Body Work

Cooper, Andrew, "*Playing in the Zone: Exploring the Spiritual Dimensions of Sports*",
Shambhala, Boston & New York, 1998.

De Ropp, Robert S., "*Sex Energy: The Sexual Force in Man and Animals*", A Delta Book, New York, 1969.

Elson, Lawrence & Wynn, Kapit, "*The Anatomy Coloring Book*", Harper & Row Publishers, New York, 1977.

Gandevia, Simon C. & Paul W. Hodges, "*Changes in Intra Abdominal Pressure During Postural
and Respiratory Activation of the Human Diaphragm*", Journal of Applied Physiology 89-967-976, 2000.

Hanna, Thomas, "*The Body of Life: Creating New Pathways for Sensory Awareness and Fluid Movement*",
Healing Arts Press, Rochester, Vermont, 1979.

Hanna, Thomas, "*Somatics: Reawakening the Mind's Control of Movement, Flexibility and Health*",
DaCapo Press, Cambridge, MA, 1988.

Hartley, Linda, "*Wisdom of the Body Moving: An Introduction to Body-Mind Centering*",
North Atlantic Books, Berkeley, CA, 1989.

Heller, Joseph & Henkin, William A., "*Body Wise: Regaining Your Natural Flexibility and Vitality
for Maximum Well-Being*", Jeremy P. Tarcher, Inc., Los Angeles, 1986.

Juhan, Deane, "*Job's Body: A Handbook for Bodywork*", Station Hill Press, Barrytown, New York, 1987.

Keleman, Stanley, "*The Human Ground: Energetic Concepts of Grounding*",
Lodestar Press, San Francisco, 1973.

Keleman, Stanley, "*Sexuality, Self & Survival*", Lodestar Press, San Francisco, CA, 1971.

Leonard, George, "*Mastery: The Keys to Success and Long-Term Fulfillment*",
A Plume Book, New York, NY, 1992.

Lowen, Alexander, "*Physical Dynamics of Character Structure: Bodily Form and Movement
in Analytic Therapy*", Grune & Stratton, New York and London, 1958.

Maisel, Edward, ed.,"*The Resurrection of the Body: The Essential Writings of F. Matthias Alexander*",
Shambhala, Boston & London, 1986.

McGill, Stuart, "*Low Back Disorders: Evidence-Based Prevention and Rehabilitation*",
Human Kinetics, Waterloo, Canada, 2002.

Murphy, Michael, "*In the Zone, Transcendent Experience in Sports*", Penguin, New York, NY, 1995.

Murphy, Michael, "*The Future of the Body: Explorations Into the Further Evolution of Human Nature*",
Putnam Publishing Group, New York, 1993.

Reich, Wilhelm, "*The Discovery of the Orgone & The Function of the Orgasm*",
The Noonday Press, New York, 1942.

Rolf, Ida P., Ph.D., "*Rolfing, The Integration of Human Structures*", Harper & Row, New York, 1977.

Scaravelli, Vanda, "*Awakening the Spine: The Stress-Free New Yoga that Works with the Body
to Restore Health, Vitality and Energy*", HarperCollins, New York, NY, 1991.

Selye, Hans, M.D., "*Stress Without Distress: How to Use Stress as a Positive Force to Achieve a Rewarding Life Style*", A Signet Book, New York, NY, 1975.

Selye, Hans, M.D., "*The Stress of Life*", McGraw-Hill Book Company, New York, Toronto & London, 1950

Todd, Mabel Elsworth, "*The Thinking Body: A Study of the Balancing Forces of Dynamic Man*", Dance Horizons, Incorporated, New York, 1937.

White, Rhea A., "*In the Zone: Transcendent Experience in Sports*", Penguin, New York, NY, 1995.

Weil, Andrew, M.D., "*Health and Healing: A New look at Medical Practices-From Folk Remedies to Chemotherapy - and What They Tell Us About*", Houghton Mifflin Company, Boston, 1983.

Weil, Andrew, M.D., "*Spontaneous Healing: How to Discover and Enhance Your Body's Natural Ability to Maintain and Heal Itself*", Alfred A. Knopf, New York, 1995.

Oriental Medicine and Health

Bisio, Tom, "*A Tooth From the Tiger's Mouth: How to Treat Your Injuries with Powerful Healing Secrets of the Great Chinese Warriors*", Simon & Schuster, New York, 2004.

Cao, Xi Zhen, "*The Massotherapy of Traditional Chinese Medicine*", Hai Feng Publishing Company, Hong Kong, 1985.

Chia, Mantak, "*Iron Shirt Chi Kung I*", Healing Tao Books, Huntington, New York, 1986.

Cohen, Kenneth S., "*The Way of Qigong: The Art and Science of Chinese Energy Healing*", Ballantine Books, New York, 1997.

Eisenberg, David, M.D., "*Encounters With Qi: Exploring Chinese Medicine*", Penguin Books, New York, NY, 1985.

Heroldova, Dana, trans., "*Acupuncture And Moxibustion, Part 1*", Oriental Institute in Academia, Publishing House of the Czechoslovak Academy of Sciences, Prague, 1968.

Kaku, Kouzo, "*The Mysterious Power of Ki: An Illustrated Account of the History and Practice of Ki in Japanese Culture*", Global Oriental, Folkestone, Kent, U.K., 2000.

Kaptchuk, Ted J., O.M.D., "*The Web That Has No Weaver: Understanding Chinese Medicine*", Congdon & Weed, New York, 1983.

Mann, M.B., Felix, "*Acupuncture: The Ancient Chinese Art of Healing*", Vintage Books Edition, New York, 1972.

Ni, Maoshing, "*The Yellow Emperor's Classic of Medicine. The Essential Text of Chinese Health and Healing*", Shambhala, Boston and London, 1995.

Toguchi, Masaru & Warren, Frank Z., M.D., "*The Complete Guide to Acupuncture and Acupressure*", Gramercy Publishing Company, New York, 1985.

Veith, Ilza, trans., "*The Yellow Emperor's Classic of Internal Medicine*", University of California Press, Berkeley, CA, 1972.

Wu, Kuang-Ming, "*On Chinese Body Thinking: A Cultural Hermeneutic*", Brill, Leiden, New York, Koln, 199

Yang, Jwing-Ming Ph.D., "*Muscle/Tendon Changing and Marrow/Brain Washing Chi Kung: The Secret of Youth*", YMAA Publication Center, MA, 1989.

Zi, Nancy, "*The Art of Breathing*", North Atlantic Books, Berkeley, CA, 2000.

Oriental Philosophies: Daoism and Bhuddism

Beck, Charlotte Joko, "*Everyday Zen, Love & Work*" Harper & Row, New York, 1989.

Blofeld, John, "*Bodhisattva of Compassion: The Mystical Tradition of Kuan Yin*", Shambhala, Boulder, 1978.

Blofeld, John, "*Taoism: The Road to Immortality*", Shambhala, Boston, 1985.

Blofeld, John, "*Taoist Mysteries and Magic*", Shambhala, Boulder, 1982.

Chang, Jolan, "*The Tao of Love and Sex: The Ancient Chinese Way to Ecstasy*", E.P. Dutton & Company, New York, 1977.

Chang, Po-Tuan, "*The Inner Teachings of Taoism*", Shambhala, Boston & London, 1986.

Chang, Chung-yuan, "*Creativity and Taoism: A Study of Chinese Philosophy, Art, and Poetry*", Harper Colophon Books, New York, 1963.

Chia, Mantak & Winn, Michael, "*Taoist Secrets of Love: Cultivating Male Sexual Energy*", Aurora Press, New York, New York, 1984.

Cleary, Thomas, "*The Secret of the Golden Flower: The Classic Chinese Book of Life*", Harper San Francisco, San Francisco, 1991.

Cleary, Thomas, trans., "*No Barrier: Unlocking the Zen Koan*", Aquarian Press, New York, 1993.

Cleary, Thomas, trans., "*Thunder in the Sky: Secrets on the Acquisition and Exercise of Power*", Shambhala, Boston & London, 1994.

Cleary, Thomas, trans., "*The Art of War by Sun Tzu*", Shambhala, Boston & Shaftesbury, 1988.

Cleary, Thomas, trans., "*Immortal Sisters: Secrets of Taoist Women*", Shambhala, Boston & Shaftesbury, 1989.

Cleary, Thomas, trans., "*Wen-Tzu: Understanding the Mysteries*", Shambhala, Boston & London, 1992.

Cleary, Thomas, trans., "*The Sutra of Hui-Neng Grand Master of Zen*", Shambhala, Boston & London, 1998.

Cleary, Thomas, trans., "*Zen Dawn: Early Zen Texts from Tun Huang*", Shambhala, Boston & London, 1986.

Cleary, Thomas, trans., "*Buddhist Yoga: A Comprehensive Course*", Shambhala, Boston & London, 1995.

Cleary, Thomas, trans.& ed., "*Vitality, Energy, Spirit: A Taoist Source Book*", Shambhala, Boston & London, 1991.

Conze, Edward, "*Buddhism: Its Essence and Development*", Harper Torchbooks, New York, 1959.

Conze, Edward, trans., "*Buddhist Scriptures*", Penguin Books, Baltimore, MD, 1959.

Conze, Edward, trans., "*Buddhist Meditation*", Harper & Row, New York, NY, 1975.

Conze, Edward, transl., "*Buddhist Texts Through the Ages*", Harper Torchbooks, New York, 1964.

Fronsdal, Gil, "*Voices From Spirit Rock: Talks on Mindfulness Practice by the Spirit Rock Teaching Collective*", Clear & Present Graphics, Rancho Cordova, CA, 1996.

Goldstein, Joseph & Kornfield, Jack, "*Seeking the Heart of Wisdom: The Path of Insight Meditation*", Shambhala, Boston & London, 1987.

Goodman, Michael Harris, "*The Last Dalai Lama: A Biography*", Shambhala, Boston, 1987.

Guenther, Herbert V., trans., "*Mind In Buddhist Psychology*", Dharma Publishing, Emeryville, CA, 1975.

Hong, Frederick & Fung, George D., trans., "*Pristine Orthodox Dharma*", Buddha's Universal Church, San Francisco, CA, 1977.

Hua, Master Tripitaka, "*The Sixth Patriarch's Dharma Jewel Platform Sutra*", Sino American Buddhist Association, San Francisco, CA, 1977.

Hua, Master Hsuan, "*The Ten Dharma-Realms Are Not Beyond A Single Thought*", Dharma Realm Buddhist Association, USA, 1976.

Huang, Po, "*The Zen Teaching of Huang Po: On The Transmission of Mind*", Grove Weidenfeld, New York, 1958.

Humana, Charles & Wu Wang, "*The Ying Yang: The Chinese Way of Love*", Avon Books, New York, New York, 1971.

Ishihara, Akira & Levy, Howard S., "*The Tao of Sex: A Chinese Introduction to the Bedroom Arts*", Harper & Row, Publishers, New York, 1968.

Lama, Dalai, "*The Universe In a Single Atom: The Convergence of Science and Spirituality*", Morgan Road Books, New York, 2005.

Leigh, William S., "*A Zen Approach to Body Therapy: From Rolf to Feldenkrais to Tanouye Roshi*", Institute of Zen Studies, Honolulu, Hawaii, 1987.

Lin, Yutang, "*The Wisdom of Laotse*", The Modern Library, New York, 1948.

Mair, Victor H., trans., "*Wandering on the Way: Early Taoist Tales and Parables of Chuang Tzu*", Bantam Book, New York, 1994.

McNaughton, William, "*The Taoist Vision*", The University of Michigan Press, Michigan, 1973.

Merton, Thomas, "*The Way of Chuang Tzu*", New Directions, New York, 1965.

Mitchell, Stephen, "*Tao Te Ching: A New English Version*", Harper & Row, Publishers, New York, 1988.

Mitchell, Stephen, ed., "*The Enlightened Heart: An Anthology of Sacred Poetry*", Harper & Row, New York, 1989.

Mitchell, Stephen, ed., "*Dropping Ashes on the Buddha: The Teaching of Zen Master Seung Sahn*", Grove Press, New York, 1976.

Morris, Vince, "*Zanshin: Meditation and the Mind in Modern Martial Arts*", Samuel Weiser, Inc., York Beach, Maine, 1992.

Price, A.F., & Mou-lam Wong, trans., "*The Diamond Sutra & the Sutra of Hui-Neng*", Shambhala, Boston, 199

Rinpoche, Sogyal, "*The Tibetan Book of Living and Dying*", Harper, San Francisco, New York, 1993.

Ross, Nancy Wilson, ed.,"*The World of Zen: An East-West Anthology*", Vintage Books, New York, 1960.

Saunders, E. Dale, "*Mudra: A Study of Symbolic Gestures in Japanese Buddhist Sculpture*", Princeton University Press, Princeton, NJ, 1985.

Schonberger, Martin, "*The I Ching & the Genetic Code: The Hidden Key to Life*", ASI Publishers Inc., New York, New York, 1979.

Siu, R.G.H., "*Ch'i: A Neo-Taoist Approach to Life*", MIT Press, Cambridge, Massachusetts, 1974.

Tainer, Steven & Belyea, Charles, "*Dragon's Play: A New Taoist Transmission of the Complete Experience of Human Life*", Great Circle Lifeworks, Berkeley, 1991.

Tsai, Chih Chung, "*Zhuangzi Speaks: The Music of Nature*", Princeton University Press, Princeton, New Jersey, 1992.

Van de Wetering, Jan Willem, "*The Empty Mirror: Experiences in a Japanese Zen Monastery*", Washington Square Press, New York, NY, 1973.

Walker, Brian & Hua Hu Ching, "*The Unknown Teaching of Lao Tzu*", Harper San Francisco, San Francisco, 1992.

Watts, Alan, "*The Way of Zen*", Vintage Books, New York, 1957.

Watts, Alan, "*The Essence of Alan Watts*", Celestial Arts, Millbrae, CA, 1974.

Watts, Alan, "*OM Creative Meditations*", Celestial Arts, Berkeley, CA, 1980.

Welch, Holmes, "*Taoism: The Parting of the Way*", Beacon Press, Boston, 1957.

Wilhelm, Richard, ed., "*The Secret of the Golden Flower: A Chinese Book of Life*", A Harvest Book, New York, 1962.

Wilhelm, Richard, & Baynes, Cary F., trans., "*The I Ching, or Book of Changes*", Princeton University Press, New York, NY, 1950.

Wong, Eva, trans., "*Seven Taoist Masters: A Folk Novel of China*", Shambhala, Boston, 1960.

Wray, Elizabeth & Rosenfield, Clare , "*The Lives of the Buddha: Siamese Temple Painting and Jataka Tales*", Weatherhill, Inc., New York, 1972.

Wright, Arthur F., "*Buddhism in Chinese History*", Stanford University Press, Stanford, CA, 1959.

Wu, Kuang-Ming, "*The Butterfly as Companion: Meditations on the First Three Chapters of the Chuang Tzu*", State University of New York Press, New York, 1990.

Neuroscience, Psychology, Mind and Spirit

Austin, James H., M.D., "*Zen and the Brain: Toward an Understanding of Meditation and Consciousness*", The MIT Press, Cambridge, MA, 1998.

Beck, Deva, R.N., "*The Pleasure Connection: How Endorphins Affect Our Health and Happiness*", Synthesis Press, San Marcos, CA, 1987.

Becker, Robert O., M.D., & Selden, Gary, "*The Body Electric: Electromagnetism and the Foundation of Li*" Quill, New York, 1985.

Becker, Robert O., M.D., "*Cross Currents: The Perils of Electro-pollution; The Promise of Electro-medicir*" Jeremy P. Tarcher, Inc., Los Angeles, 1990.

Begley, Sharon, "*Train Your Mind, Change Your Brain: How a New Science Reveals Our Extraordinary Potential to Transform Ourselves*", Ballantine Books, New York, 2007.

Benson, Herbert, M.D., "*Timeless Healing: The Power of Biology and Belief*", Fireside, New York, NY, 199[...]

Blakeslee, Thomas R., "*The Right Brain: A New Understanding of the Unconscious Mind and It's Creative Powers*", Anchor Press/Doubleday, Garden City, NY, 1980.

Blakeslee, Sandra and Blakely, Thomas, "*The Body Has a Mind of Its Own: How Body Maps in Your Brain Help You Do (Almost) Everything Better*", Random House, New York, 2008.

Brown, Norman O., "*Life Against Death: The Psychoanalytical Meaning of History*", Vintage Books, New York, 1959.

Brown, Norman O., "*Love's Body*", Vintage Books, New York, 1966.

Calder, Nigel, "*The Mind of Man: From New Haven to New Delhi–a Worldwide Report on the Drama of Brain Research*", The Viking Press, New York, 1970.

Conway, Flo, & Siegelman, Jim , "*Snapping: America's Epidemic of Sudden Personality Change*", J.B. Lippincott Company, Philadelphia and New York, 1978.

d'Aquili, Eugene & Newberg, Andrew B., "*The Mystical Mind: Probing the Biology of Religious Experienc*" Fortress Press, Minneapolis, 1999.

d'Aquili, Eugene & Laughlin, Charles D., Jr., "*Brain, Symbol & Experience: Toward a Neuro-Phenomenolo* *of Human Consciousness*", New Science Library, Boston, MA, 1990.

d'Aquili, Eugene, M.D. & Newberg, Andrew, Ph.D., M.D., "*Why God Won't Go Away: Brain Science & the Biology of Belief*", Ballantine Books, New York, 2001.

Damasio, Antonio, "*Looking for Spinoza: Joy, Sorrow, and the Feeling Brain*", Harcourt, Inc., Orlando, Florida, 2003.

Damasio, Antonio, "*The Feeling of What Happens: Body and Emotion in the Making of Consciousness*", Harcourt Brace & Company, New York, 1999.

De Bono, Edward, "*The Mechanism of Mind*", Penguin Books, Middlesex, England, 1969.

De Gelder, Beatrice, ed., & de Haan, Edward H.F., eds., "*Out of Mind: Varieties of Unconscious Processe*" Oxford University Press, New York, 2001.

De Gelder, Beatrice, ed., "*Knowledge and Representation*", Routledge & Kegan, London, 1982.

De Ropp, Robert S., "*Drugs and the Mind*", Grove Press, New York, 1957.

Dychtwald, Ken, "*Body-Mind*", A Jove Book, New York, 1978.

Feinberg, Todd E., M.D., "*Altered Egos: How the Brain Creates the Self*", Oxford University Press, New York, 200[...]

Feldenkrais, Moshe, "*Awareness Through Movement: Health Exercises for Personal Growth*", Harper San Francisco, San Francisco, 1972.

Gladwell, Malcolm, "*Blink: The Power of Thinking Without Thinking*", Little, Brown and Company, New York, 2005.

Gladwell, Malcolm, "*Outliers: The Story of Success*", Little, Brown and Company, New York, 2008.

Gooch, Stan, "*The Double Helix of the Mind*", Wildwood House, London, 1980.

Hampden-Turner, Charles, "*Maps of the Mind: Charts and Concepts of the Mind and Its Labyrinths*", Collier Books, New York, 1981.

Hooper, Judith & Teresi, Dick, "*The 3-Pound Universe: the Brain, From the Chemistry of the Mind to the New Frontiers of the Soul*", Dell Publishing Co., Inc., New York, New York, 1986.

Hull, R.F.C., & Jacobi, Jolande, eds., "*C.G. Jung: Psychological Reflections; A New Anthology of His Writings 1905-1961*", Princeton University Press, New Jersey, 1973.

Huxley, Aldous, "*The Doors of Perception and Heaven and Hell*", Flamingo, Hammersmith, London, 1994.

Jaffe, Aniela, trans., "*C.G. Jung Word and Image*", Princeton University Press, Princeton, 1979.

Jung, Emma, "*Animus and Anima: Two Essays*", Spring Publications, Zurich, Switzerland, 1957.

Jung, C.G., "*Analytical Psychology: Its Theory & Practice*", Random House, Inc., New York, 1970.

Jung, C.G., "*Memories, Dreams, Reflections*", Vintage Books, New York, 1961.

Keleman, Stanley, "*Your Body Speaks its Mind*", Center Press, Berkeley, CA, 1975.

Llinas, Rodolfo R., "*i of the Vortex: From Neurons to Self*", A Bradford Book, The MIT Press, Massachusetts, 2001.

McCrone, John, "*Going Inside: A Tour Round a Single Moment of Consciousness*", Fromm International, New York, 2001.

Milgram, Stanley, "*Obedience to Authority*", Harper & Row, New York, 1969.

Montagu, Ashley, "*The Natural Superiority of Women*", Collier Books, New York, 1952.

Norretranders, Tor, "*The User Illusion: Cutting Consciousness Down to Size*", Viking, New York, NY, 1991.

Ornstein, Robert E., "*The Nature of Human Consciousness: A Book of Readings*", W. H. Freeman and Company, San Francisco, CA, 1973.

Ornstein, Robert E., "*The Psychology of Consciousness*", Penguin Books, New York, 1972.

Ornstein, Robert E., "*On the Experience of Time*", Penguin Books, New York, 1975.

Pert, Candace B., PhD, "*Molecules of Emotion: Why You feel the Way You Feel*", Scribner, New York, NY, 1997.

Ratey, John J., M.D., "*A User's Guide to the Brain: Perception, Attention, and the Four Theaters of the Brain*", Vintage Books, New York, 2002.

Sacks, Oliver, "*Musicophilia: Tales of Music and the Brain*", Alfred A. Knopf, New York, 2007.

Sargant, William, *"Battle for the Mind: A Physiology of Conversion and Brainwashing"*,
Perennial Library, New York, 1971.

Schwarz, Jack, *"Voluntary Controls: Exercises for Creative Meditation and for Activating the Potential of the Chakras"*, E.P. Dutton, New York, 1978.

Snyder, Solomon H., M.D., *"Madness and the Brain"*, McGraw-Hill, New York, 1974.

Von Franz, Marie-Louise, Dr., *"The Way of the Dream"*, Windrose Films Ltd., Toronto, Ontario, Canada, 1988.

Von Franz, Marie-Louise, *"Number and Time: Reflections Leading Toward a Unification of Depth Psychology and Physics"*, Northwestern University Press, Evanston, 1974.

Wilber, Ken, ed., *"The Holographic Paradigm and Other Paradoxes: Exploring the Leading Edge of Science"*, Shambhala, Boulder & London, 1982.

Parabola: The Magazine of Myth and Tradition, *"Time & Presence"*, Fifteenth Anniversary Issue, Society for the Study of Myth and Tradition, Inc., New York, Volume XV, Number 1, February, 1990.

Parabola: The Magazine of Myth and Tradition, *"Attention"*, Society for the Study of Myth and Tradition, Inc., New York, Volume XV, Number 2, May, 1990.

Oriental Culture and History

Benoit, Herbert, *"The Supreme Doctrine: Psychological Studies in Zen Thought"*, The Viking Press, New York, 1955.

Cohen, Paul A., *"History in Three Keys: The Boxers as Event, Experience, and Myth"*, Columbia University Press, New York, 1997.

de Bary, Wm. Theodore, ed., *"Sources of Chinese Tradition, Volume 1: Introduction to Oriental Civilizations"*, Columbia University Press, New York and London, 1960.

de Mente, Boyé Lafayette, *"The Chinese Have a Word for It: The Complete Guide to Chinese Thought and Culture"*, Passport Books, NTC/Contemporary Publishing Group, Inc., Chicago, Il, 2000.

Ebrey, Patricia Buckley, ed., *"Chinese Civilization: A Sourcebook"*, The Free Press, New York, NY, 1993.

Eliade, Mircea, *"Cosmos And History: The Myth of the Eternal Return"*, Harper Torchbooks, New York, 1954.

Ellis, Andrew & Wiseman, Nigel, *"Grasping the Wind: An Exploration Into the Meaning of Chinese Acupuncture Point Names"*, Paradigm Publications, Brookline, MA, 1989.

Lin, Yutang, ed., *"The Wisdom of Confucius"*, Illustrated Modern Library, USA, 1943.

Liu, Xinru, *"Ancient India and Ancient China: Trade and Religious Exchanges AD 1-600"*, Oxford University Press, Bombay, Calcutta, Madras, 1994.

Moyers, Bill, *"Healing and The Mind"*, Doubleday, New York, 1993.

Needham, Joseph, *"The Grand Titration: Science and Society in East and West"*, George Allen & Unwin, London, 1969.

Polatin, Betsy, "*Macrobiotics in Motion: Yin & Yang in Moving Spirals*", Japan Publications, Inc., Tokyo and New York, 1987.

Porter, Bill, "*Road to Heaven: Encounters With Chinese Hermits*", Mercury House, San Francisco, CA, 1993.

Powell, James N., "*The Tao of Symbols: How to Transcend the Limits of our Symbolism*", Quill, New York, 1982.

Waley, Arthur, "*Three Ways of Thought in Ancient China*", Doubleday Anchor Books, Garden City, NY, 1939.

Weber, Max, "*The Religion of China*", The Free Press Of Glencoe, USA, 1951.

Western Science and Philosophy

Abrams, Nancy & Primack, Joel R., "*The View from the Center of the Universe: Discovering Our Extraordinary Place in the Cosmos*", Riverhead Books, New York, 2006.

Bentov, Itzhak, "*A Cosmic Book: On the Mechanics of Creation*", E.P. Dutton, New York, 1982.

Blair, Lawrence, "*Rhythms of Vision: The Changing Patterns of Belief*", Schocken Books, New York, 1975.

Campbell, Joseph, "*Transformations of Myth Through Time*", Harper & Row, New York, 1990.

Capra, Fritjof, "*The Tao of Physics: An Exploration of the Parallels Between Modern Physics and Eastern Mysticism*", Shambhala, Boulder, 1975.

Darwin, Charles, "*The Expression of the Emotions in Man and Animals ('Introduction, Afterword and Commentaries by Paul Ekman')*", Oxford University Press, Oxford, 1998.

Doczi, Gyorgy, "*The Power of Limits: Proportional Harmonies in Nature, Art and Architecture*", Shambhala, Boulder & London, 1981.

Ekman, Paul, "*Emotions Revealed: Recognizing Faces and Feelings to Improve Communication and Emotional Life*", Times Books, New York, 2003.

Greenstein, George, "*Symbiotic Universe: Life and the Cosmos in Unity*", William Morrow and Company, Inc., New York, 1988.

Gribbin, John, "*Time Warps: Is Time Travel Possible?*", Dell Publishing Co., Inc., New York, New York, 1979.

Hayward, Jeremy W., "*Shifting Worlds, Changing Minds: Where the Sciences and Buddhism Meet*", Shambhala, Boston & London, 1987.

Hofstadter, Douglas R. & Dennett, Daniel C., "*The Mind's I: Fantasies and Reflections on Self and Soul*", Bantam Books, Toronto, 1981.

Holbrook, Bruce, "*The Stone Monkey: An Alternative Chinese-Scientific Reality*", William Morrow and Company, Inc., New York, 1981.

Huizinga, Johan, "*Homo Ludens: A Study of the Play Element in Culture*", The Beacon Press, Boston, 1950.

Lakoff, George & Johnson, Mark , "*Metaphors We Live By*", University of Chicago Press, Chicago, 1980.

Lakoff, George & Johnson, Mark, "*Philosophy in the Flesh: The Embodied Mind and its Challenge to Western Thought*", Basic Books, Perseus Book Group, New York, 1999.

McClain, Ernest G., "*The Myth of Invariance: The Origin of the Gods, Mathematics and Music From the Rg Veda to Plato*", Shambhala, Boulder & London, 1978.

Merleau-Ponty, Maurice, "*Phenomenology of Perception*", Routledge & Kegan Paul, London, 1962.

Narby, Jeremy, "*Intelligence in Nature: An Inquiry Into Knowledge*", Jeremy P. Tarcher, Penguin, New York, 2005.

Sartre, Jean-Paul, "*Being and Nothingness: An Essay on Phenomenological Ontology*", Philosophical Library, New York, New York, 1956.

Sheldrake, Rupert, "*The Sense of Being Stared At: And Other Aspects of the Extended Mind*", Crown Publishers, New York, 2003.

Sheldrake, Rupert, "*The Rebirth of Nature: The Greening of Science and God*", Century, London, 1990.

Sheldrake, Rupert, "*A New Science of Life: The Hypothesis of Formative Causation*", J.P. Tarcher, Inc, Los Angeles, CA, 1981.

Shlain, Leonard, "*Art & Physics: Parallel Vision in Space, Time, and Light*", Harper Perennial, New York, 1991.

Sinnott, Edmund W., "*Cell & Psyche: The Biology of Purpose*", Harper Torchbooks, Harper & Row, 1950

Sinnott, Edmund W., "*The Biology of the Spirit*", Viking Press, New York, 1955.

Thomas, Lewis, "*The Lives of a Cell: Notes of a Biology Watcher*", Bantam Books, Inc., Toronto/New York/London, 1974.

Young, Arthur, "*The Reflexive Universe: Evolution of Consciousness*", Delacorte Press, 1976.

Zukav, Gary, "*The Dancing Wu Li Masters: An Overview of the New Physics*", William Morrow and Company, Inc., New York, 1979.

Index

A

Accommodation/withdrawal reflex, **62–64**, *63*, 65, 109, 135, 136

Alerting reflex, 56

Amoeba, 22, 67, *67*

Arcuate line, 73, *73*

Athletes (mystics of body), 113, 144, **147–150**, *147,* 151, *154,* 156

Attention
  listening, 128, 130, 171
  shifting, 111

Attention association area (aaa)
  abstractions, 95, 104, 106, 108
  explained, 96, 107
  figure, *92*
  transcendent experiences, 151, 152, 153
  yi, 104, 106, 107, 108, 151, 152, 153
  see also Frontal lobes

Attention-intention. *see* Intention-attention

Awareness
  of balance, proprioception, and central equilibrium, 21, 31, 44–46, 58, 98, 160
  carefulness, 47
  of the center, 54, 69, 121
  enlightened, 137, 159–160, 171
  and faps, 100
  focus, 16, 44–46, 109, 142, 155–156
  and the frame, 83, 84, 87, 110, 117, 121, 123
  vs. ignorance, 161
  integration of, 44–46, 90
  and jin, 90, 100, 112
  making the involuntary voluntary, 30–31, 55, 57, 58, 60, 63, 65, 70, 109
  martial asset, 17, 21, 73, 87, 89, 90, 161, 163, 166
  in movement and stillness, 24, 31, 33–54, 56
  neurology of, 95, 96, 98, 99
  neurology of, frontal lobes, 21, 93, 144, 149, 161
  neurology of, parietal lobes, 141, 142, 144, 149, 161
  and no-force, 15, 17, 90, 163
  perceptual, as yin, 15, 126
  of peri-personal space, 157
  peripheral training, 165
  pre-cognition, 118, 149
  of pressure and distance, 130

H

I

M

P